MARIUSZ ROZYCKI

THREE SEAS INITIATIVE & CENTRAL EUROPE

LONDON, 09/2022

Table of Contents

INTRODUCTION 5

PART 1 - The Three Seas Initiative (3SI) in 2022 8

Chapter 1 – The 3SI Fund 8

Chapter 2 – The 3SI projects 10

Chapter 3 – The 12 3SI countries 18

    Austria 21
    Bulgaria 23
    Croatia 25
    Czechia 27
    Estonia 29
    Hungary 31
    Latvia 33
    Lithuania 35
    Poland 36
    Romania 40
    Slovakia 42
    Slovenia 44

Chapter 4 – Digital 3SI 46

Chapter 5 – Energy 3SI 48

Chapter 6 – Transport 3SI 50

PART 2 - The 3SI – US & UK Engagement 52

Chapter 1 - 3SI – US Engagement 52

Chapter 2 - 3SI – UK Engagement 64

Chapter 3 - 3SI & Germany 76

Chapter 4 - 3SI & China 87

Chapter 5 - 3SI & Russia 103

Part 3 - CENTRAL EUROPE - Historical background 114

Chapter 1 – Amber Road 114

Chapter 2 – Christianity 121

Chapter 3 – Central Europe in XV century 133

Chapter 4 – Central Europe in XVI century 145

Chapter 5 – Central Europe in XVII century 154

Chapter 6 – Central Europe in XVIII century 164

Chapter 7 - Central Europe in XIX century 169

Chapter 8 - Central Europe in XX century 174

Chapter 9 – New Intermarium (XXI century) 192

PART 4 Extras 197

MAPS 197

More about the Three Seas Initiative and Central Europe on my blog:

www.mariuszrozycki.co.uk

I dedicate this book to my beloved parents, who are always in my mind.

Mariusz Rozycki

Therefore, since we are justified by faith, we have peace with God through our Lord Jesus Christ. Through him we have obtained access to this grace in which we stand, and we rejoice in our hope of sharing the glory of God. More than that, we rejoice in our sufferings, knowing that suffering produces endurance, and endurance produces character, and character produces hope, and hope does not disappoint us, because God's love has been poured into our hearts through the Holy Spirit who has been given to us.

Romans 5

"To know that we know what we know, and to know that we do not know what we do not know, that is true knowledge."

Nicolaus Copernicus

INTRODUCTION

The Three Seas Initiative (3SI) project was presented first time after the presidential elections in Poland in 2015. In his speech, new elected president Andrzej Duda pointed to the proposals for the renewal of the Visegrad Group and closer cooperation among the Central and Eastern Europe countries. The new platform of cooperation was called the Three Seas Initiative (3SI). Events unfolded rapidly, and a summit initiating cooperation under the Three Seas Initiative took place less than a year later, at the end of August 2016, in Dubrovnik, Croatia. Another, very important meeting of the Three Seas countries took place at the beginning of July 2017 at the Royal Castle in Warsaw. US President Donald Trump participated in the summit, giving a clear signal to the twelve countries involved that the initiative had received political support from the United States. At the same time, the framework for the future cooperation of the Three Seas Initiative was quite precisely defined. It was indicated that by integrating the region and tightening cooperation between a group of countries, European integration will be strengthened, and the structural funds will be the instrument to implement this concept. In other words - connecting the region anew with new routes running directly from the North to the South, from the Baltic Sea to the Black Sea and the Adriatic Sea will boost trade and build new economic ties between the countries and enterprises of the region in digital, trade, and energy sectors.

Since that several 3SI summits took place:

2016 – Dubrovnik, Croatia

2017 – Warsaw, Poland

2018 – Bucharest, Romania

2019 – Ljubljana, Slovenia
2020 – Tallinn, Estonia
2021 – Sofia, Bulgaria
2022 – Riga, Latvia

There has been increasing meaning of Central Europe in the world since the collapse the Soviet Union and communism in 1989/1991. From a peripheral, and poor region of countries that struggled to survive between Russia and Germany, it has been more reach and more open to the world, absorbing more investments, tourists, workers, and technologies. Central Europe in 1990s wanted to be a part of the West, in 2000s enjoyed integration with NATO and the EU, in 2010s begun searching own model of development, which resulted in the Tree Seas Initiative.

Great English thinker Halford Mackinder who found geopolitics always emphasised how important is the role of Central and Eastern Europe in world politics. He wrote: "Whoever reigns in Eastern Europe - reigns over the heart of Eurasia. Whoever rules over the heart of Eurasia rules over a world island. Whoever rules over a world island rules over the world."

The world changes as well as the region that has ambition to be one of the most important parts of the globe. It just the beginning of the 3SI project which may not develop as fast as we hope without an engagement of a powerful economies such as the US or UK. This has been considered in part 2 of this book together with possible influence of countries such as Germany, China, and Russia which may not be interested in the prosperous 3SI.

When the 3SI was found many politicians ignored this project (why we need it if we have the EU), then they mocked it (who the Central Europeans think they are!), then the same people started attacking the 3SI (it is a dangerous idea that will divide

Europe!) reflection followed, and the Germans began to push themselves towards the Three Seas Initiative, seeing it as the threat to their interests.

In part 3 of the book readers can find a historical background that can help better understand how difficult was history for the region, and what economic processes through centuries shaped countries such as Poland or Hungary.

PART 1 - The Three Seas Initiative (3SI) in 2022

Chapter 1 – The 3SI Fund

The main objective of the Three Seas Fund is to invest in transport, energy and digital infrastructure on the north-south axis in the Three Seas countries and to offset the differences in the development of individual regions of the European Union.

Its role is to complement and strengthen the capital deployment of individual Three Seas countries and European Union financial instruments. The fund is a commercial and market driven initiative that will grant a diversified investment and an attractive return to the investors.

The constitutive act of the Three Seas Fund was signed by the presidents of development banks from Poland (Bank Gospodarstwa Krajowego) and Romania (Exim Bank). As an international venture, the Three Seas Fund was created under Luxembourg law, which is a renowned fund domicile for international investors.[1]

The fund is managed by supervisory board (12 members), and management board (9 members).

The core sponsors of the fund are:

Bank Gospodarstwa Krajowego (BGK) - Poland

EximBank - Romania

Altum - Latvia

Estonian Ministry of Finance - Estonia

SID Banka - Slovenia

EXIM - Hungary

Bulgarian Development Bank (BDB) - Bulgaria

---

[1] www.3siif.eu/the-fund/

Hrvatska banka za obnovu i razvitak (HBOR) - Croatia
Viešųjų investicijų plėtros agentūra (VIPA) – Lithuania

So far, after two years of activity (it started in May 2019) the 3SI Investment Fund raised a billion euros, and is planning to gain 5 billion euros by encouraging investors from Japan, South Korea, Australia.
Amber Infrastructure Group (Amber) has been appointed the exclusive Investment Adviser to the Three Seas Fund.
Amber is a specialist international investment manager, focused on investment origination, asset management and fund management. Amber has experience and expertise spanning a broad range of infrastructure sectors and geographies. With over £8 billion of assets managed, Amber invests across six funds and a number of managed accounts.
Amber's core business focuses on sourcing, developing, advising, investing in and managing infrastructure assets across the public, transport, energy, digital and demographic infrastructure sectors that support the lives of people, homes and businesses internationally. Amber adopts a full-service, sustainable approach to investments and is able to manage the entire investment lifecycle in-house.
Headquartered in London, Amber has an international presence with approximately 135 infrastructure investment professionals across Europe, North America and Australia. While Amber draws upon its broader platform to deliver the objectives of Three Seas Funds, it also has dedicated team members located across offices in the CEE region including Vienna, Warsaw and Prague.[2]

---

[2] www.3siif.eu/the-investment-adviser

Chapter 2 – The 3SI projects

3SI Projects by countries:

Bulgaria: (3)
1. Tunnel under Petrohan Pass
2. Restoration of the design parameters of Ruse-Varna railway line
3. UGS Chiren Expansion

Czechia: (1)
1. Danube – Oder – Elbe Connection

Croatia: (16)
1) Construction of A5 Motorway
2) Regulation Works on the Danube River
3) Oil and Gas Terminal in Port of Ploce
4) Rehabilitation of rail section
5) Construction of the Second Track
6) Sava IW section between Jaruge – Novi Grad
7) LNG Terminal on the Island of KRK
8) Port of Rijeka infrastructure upgrading and development, development of multimodal platforms and interconnections – Adriatic Gate container terminal (POR2CORE-AGCT)
9) Project of Rijeka - Zagreb Deep Sea Container Terminal
10) Upgrade of the Rijeka Port infrastructure – Port Community System (POR2CORE-PCS)
11) Port of Rijeka infrastructure upgrading - General cargo terminal (POR2CORE-GCT)
12) Upgrade of the Rijeka Port infrastructure - Rijeka Basin (POR2CORE-Rijeka Basin)

13) Upgrade of the Rijeka Port infrastructure - Bakar bulk cargo terminal (POR2CORE-BCTB)
14) IAP
15) NP-BBI Programme
16) Compressor Station 1 at the Croatian Gas Transmission System

Estonia: (4)
1. Rail Baltica
2. Via Baltica
3. Commissioning of the regional LNG terminal in Paldiski
4. Construction of the 500MW Estonian PHES

Hungary: (15)
1. Construction of a 2nd track between Sopron and Győr, Phase 0: Section Sopron – Harka, including capacity increase of Sopron node.
2. Construction of the Zalaszentiván (HU) triangle track
3. Reconstruction and capacity improvement of traction substations in Hungary
4. Upgrade the railway link between the inland Freeport of Budapest and the core network corridor (reconstructing the Gubacsi railway bridge and upgrading the railway connection leading to the port) – works.
5. Preparation of the electrification on Zalaszentiván – Nagykanizsa railway line (HU)
6. Construction of a new road bridge over the Tisza in the Záhony area
7. North-South Gas Corridor – Expansion of existing capacity between Hungary and Slovakia
8. ROHU – Second Phase
9. Launching a Hungarian-American pilot project in Hungary, studying the use of hydrogen

10. Extraction of unconventional gas
11. 500 MW CCGT Power Plant to replace the Marta Power Plant
12. Development of 130-260 MW PV solar power plant
13. Development of intelligent electricity networks
14. Development of High-Performance Computing (HPC) infrastructure, establishment and operation of HPC ecosystem in the CEE-n region
15. Adaption of GSM-R towers to 5G

Latvia: (8)
1. Rail Baltica
2. Development of a wind farm project
3. Introduction of smart outdoor lighting technologies
4. Development and implementation of mobility solutions
5. Construction of the Salaspils-Baltezers as part of the Via Baltica project
6. Construction of a coastal LNG terminal
7. Development of cross-border optical fibre network
8. Development of cross-border network of data centres

Lithuania: (8)
1. Gas Interconnector Republic of Poland-Republic of Lithuania (GIPL)
2. Integration and synchronisation of the Baltic States' electricity system with the European networks
3. Viking train
4. Rail Baltica
5. Via Baltica
6. Purchase of the FSRU INDEPENDENCE (Klaipėda LNG terminal)
7. 5G Cross-Border Transport Corridors for connected and automated Mobility CAM in Baltics

8. Installation of electricity storage facilities (200 MW)

Poland: (10)
1. Gas Interconnector Republic of Poland-Republic of Lithuania (GIPL)
2. Via Carpatia
3. Diversification of gas supply sources and integration of gas infrastructure in the Three Seas Region with the implementation of the Baltic Pipe project and cross-border interconnections Republic of Poland-Slovak Republic and Republic of Poland-Ukraine
4. U-space, low altitude space as a new field of economy. Central European Drone Demonstrator (CEDD)
5. Baltic – Adriatic TEN – T Core Network Corridor
6. The 3 Seas Digital Highway
7. Rail Baltica
8. 3SI Marketplace
9. "Amber" Rail Freight Corridor
10. Danube – Oder – Elbe Connection

Romania: (7)
1. BRUA
2. Transportation stock exchange in the 3SI region
3. Digital Platform on monitoring hydrographic bases in the 3SI region
4. Via Carpatia
5. FAIRway Danube
6. Rail-2-Sea "Modernization and development of railway line Gdansk(PL) – Constanța (RO)"
7. Interoperability solutions for a digitized and sustainable energy sector in the 3SI area in the field of energy storage

Slovakia: (3)

1. Eastring
2. Modernisation of railway line Devínska Nová Ves – State border SK/CZ
3. Motorway D3 Čadca, Bukov – Svrčinovec

Slovenia: (6)
1. HU-SI gas interconnector
2. Pilot Project 5G PPDR - Public Protection Disaster Relief
3. SINCRO.GRID
4. Construction of the 2nd railway track between Koper and Divača
5. Reconstruction of the Ljubljana railway junction (LRJ)
6. Adria Flood and Drought Risk Mitigation System

All 3SI projects by type: Transport 49%, Energy 37%, Digital 14%

No. of projects per country (January 2022)

Hungary - 17
Croatia - 17
Poland - 12
Lithuania - 11
Latvia - 10
Slovakia - 8
Slovenia - 7
Romania - 7
Estonia - 6
Bulgaria - 4
Czechia – 1

The majority of the funding for the 81 priority projects is planned to come from national and EU sources to the volume of up to 2/3 or 65% of all €179.3 bln needed, of which 53% is reported as already secured. 60% of the investment is expected to come from national funding or other EU funds, 20% - from 3SIIF, 10% from EIB, and the remaining 10% from other sources.

Case studies (examples of completed 3SI projects):

Case 1: Compressor station 1 at the Croatian gas transmission system. Total cost: 25 million Euro. 100% financed by the 3SIIF.

The construction of the „Compressor station 1" at the Croatian gas transmission system, together with the implementation of the phase I and the construction of the connecting gas pipeline Omišalj-Zlobin will provide the transport of gas in the direction of Hungary by the existing 75-bar system with an annual capacity of 1,7 bcma.
Compressor stations will significantly increase the efficiency of the Croatian gas transmission system. Compressor stations are an integral part of the transmission system, integrated in a way that increases the flexibility in managing the existing transmission capacities of the system and provides rational increase of transmission capacities according to user needs, which are the requirements of the market, as well as satisfy market conditions arising from the application of new legal regulation.

Case 2: Project of Rijeka - Zagreb Deep Sea Container Terminal. Total cost: 265 million Euro. Financed in 40% by the 3SIIF, and in 60% by National funding, EBRD, EIB, and EU funding.

The Port of Rijeka has experienced healthy growth of container volumes, with almost 250,000 TEU handled in 2017. The growth in the container segment has been mainly attributed to further containerization of general cargo in the region, upgraded inland and hinterland road and rail access, modernized port facilities, and improved Customs facilitation procedures that allowed the Port of Rijeka to compete against other Northern Adriatic ports for both domestic traffic and trade volumes of land locked hinterland countries.

Because of the increased trade volumes, a port modernization project (Rijeka Gateway Project) financed by the loan from the World Bank, is being implemented. The overall objective of the port component of the project is to support the transformation and modernization of the port of Rijeka, thereby increasing both its competitiveness and traffic. The project involves transforming the port from a service port model to a landlord port model, thereby increasing the private sector involvement and capital in the port. As a part of Rijeka Gateway Project, the Government of Croatia has nominated the Zagreb Deep Sea Container Terminal as Strategic Project. PRA intends to concession the operations of the Zagreb Deep Sea Container Terminal in a way that the PRA will finance the infrastructure and the Concessionaire (private investment) should finance the equipment and superstructure as well as operate and maintain the terminal facilities. The new Zagreb Deep Sea Container Terminal will have pier length of 680 m, of which PRA will finance the construction of the first 400 m, and the Concessionaire (private investment) will optionally finance an additional 280 m.

For the purpose of developing and modernizing the port of Rijeka, the concession grantor the Port of Rijeka Authority intends to ensure additional capacities for container handling in the western part of the port of Rijeka, at the location where the new Zagreb Deep Sea Container Terminal is to be built in phased manner:

Phase 1: construction of a 400 -metre quay wall with the associated landfill financed by the concession grantor based on a World Bank's loan. The new pier shall be adequate for latest generation of container ships.

Phase 1A: construction of terminal infrastructure and superstructure and installation of terminal equipment to be financed based on the concessionaire's capital investment.

Phase 2: construction of a 280 -metre extension of the quay wall with the associated landfill (680 m of pier in total) - option.

Chapter 3 – The 12 3SI countries

Country	% of world GDP, 2018	% of world exports, 2018	% of world imports, 2018	High technology exports, $ million, 2020	Patent applications by residents, 2019
Austria	0.46	1.03	0.99	16.0	2,066
Bulgaria	0.07	0.18	0.17	0.8	186
Croatia	0.06	0.13	0.13	1.1	195
Czechia	0.25	0.78	0.73	39.6	765
Estonia	0.03	0.09	0.09	2.2	31
Hungary	0.16	0.55	0.53	18.1	427
Latvia	0.03	0.09	0.09	1.8	82
Lithuania	0.05	0.16	0.16	2.6	90
Poland	0.60	1.32	1.27	20.3	3,887
Romania	0.24	0.41	0.45	7.0	881
Slovakia	0.11	0.41	0.41	8.0	206
Slovenia	0.05	0.19	0.17	2.5	255
3SI in total	2.11	5.34	5.19	120.0	9,071
Brazil	1.94	1.14	1.13	5.9	5,464
Russia	1.68	2.07	1.43	6.6	23,337
Japan	6.02	3.73	3.82	103.0	245,372
India	3.28	2.19	2.65	21.6	19,454

No. in the world	Country	Innovations index (0-100), 2021	No. in the world	Country	R & D expenditure, % of GDP, 2018
1	Switzerland	65.5	1	Israel	4.95
2	Sweden	63.1	2	South Korea	4.81
3	USA	61.3	3	Sweden	3.34
4	UK	59.8	4	Japan	3.26
5	South Korea	59.3	5	Austria	3.17
18	Austria	50.9	16	Slovenia	1.94
21	Estonia	49.9	17	Czechia	1.93

23	Czechia	49.0	20	Hungary	1.6
32	Slovenia	44.1	21	Estonia	1.43
34	Hungary	42.7	27	Poland	1.21
35	Bulgaria	42.4	31	Croatia	0.97
37	Slovakia	40.2	32	Lithuania	0.94
38	Latvia	40.0	35	Slovakia	0.8
39	Lithuania	39.9	36	Bulgaria	0.77
40	Poland	39.9	39	Latvia	0.63
42	Croatia	37.3	45	Romania	0.51
48	Romania	35.6	-		-	-

% of total employment in:		World Bank data	
Country	Industry	Services	Agriculture
Austria	25	71	4
Bulgaria	30	63	7
Croatia	28	66	6
Czechia	37	60	3
Estonia	29	68	3
Hungary	32	63	5
Latvia	24	69	7
Lithuania	26	68	6
Poland	32	60	8
Romania	30	49	21
Slovakia	36	61	3
Slovenia	34	62	4
3SI in average	30	63	6
Ukraine	25	61	14
Belarus	30	59	11
Moldova	22	57	21

EU	25	71	4
Brazil	20	71	9
Russia	27	67	6
China	27	47	25
Japan	24	72	3
India	25	32	43

Austria

Economic growth: 3.6% (2022)
Exports/Imports ($bln): 157/158

Main dates from history:
- Name Austria - 1 November 996
- Duchy - 17 September 1156
- Empire - 11 August 1804
- Austria-Hungary - 30 March 1867
- First Republic - 10 September 1919
- Second Republic - 27 April 1945

International rankings:
No. 21 in the World Economic Forum: Global Competitiveness Report
No. 22 in the World Economic Forum: Financial Development Index
No. 16 in the World Competitiveness Yearbook
No. 18 in the Global Innovation Index
No. 25 in the Index of Economic Freedom

Austria	Value
% of world GDP, 2018	0.46
% of world exports, 2018	1.03
% of world imports, 2018	0.99
% of world Foreign Direct Investment, 2018	-2.79
Innovations index (0-100), 2021	50.9
R & D expenditure, % of GDP, 2018	3.17
Information technology exports, % of total goods exports, 2019	3.13
High technology exports, $ million, 2020	16.00

Patent applications by residents, 2019	2.066
Wind electricity generation, billion kilowatthours, 2020	6.79
Solar electricity generation, billion kilowatthours, 2020	2.04
Hydroelectricity generation, billion kilowatthours, 2020	40.95
Renewable power generation, billion kilowatthours, 2020	54.49
Quality of air transport infrastructure, 1(low) - 7(high), 2019	5.20
Airline passengers of domestically owned airlines, mln, 2019	46.48

Bulgaria

Economic growth: 2.5% (2022)
Exports/Imports ($bln): 31/34

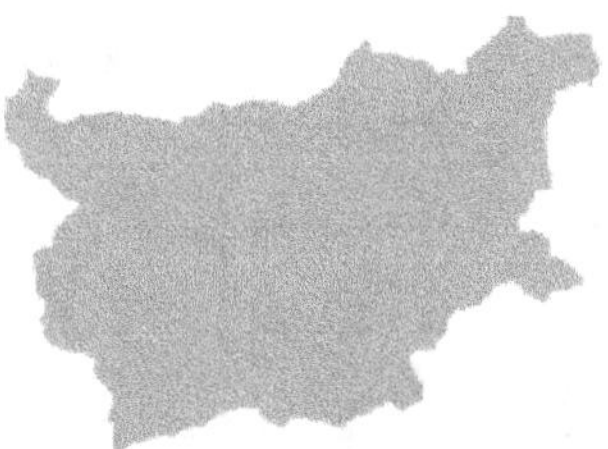

Main dates from history:
- 1st Bulgarian Empire - 681–1018
- 2nd Bulgarian Empire - 1185–1396
- Principality of Bulgaria - 3 March 1878
- Declaration of Independence - 5 October 1908
- Current republic - 15 November 1990

International rankings:
No. 28 in the Fraser Institute Economic Freedom of the World
No. 73 in the Corruption Perceptions Index
No. 62 in the World Economic Forum Global Competitiveness Report
No. 32 in the Foreign Policy Globalization Index
No. 57 in the Economist Intelligence Unit Quality-of-life Index

Bulgaria	Value
% of world GDP, 2018	0.07
% of world exports, 2018	0.18
% of world imports, 2018	0.17
% of world Foreign Direct Investment, 2018	0.18
Innovations index (0-100), 2021	42.4

R & D expenditure, % of GDP, 2018	0.77
Information technology exports, % of total goods exports, 2019	3.21
High technology exports, $ million, 2020	0.80
Patent applications by residents, 2019	186
Wind electricity generation, billion kilowatthours, 2020	1.48
Solar electricity generation, billion kilowatthours, 2020	1.47
Hydroelectricity generation, billion kilowatthours, 2020	3.35
Renewable power generation, billion kilowatthours, 2020	7.88
Quality of air transport infrastructure, 1(low) - 7(high), 2019	4.50
Airline passengers of domestically owned airlines, mln, 2019	0.83

Croatia

Economic growth: 3.4% (2022)
Exports/Imports ($bln): 17/26

Main dates from history:
- Kingdom - 925
- Personal union with Hungary - 1102
- Joined Habsburg Monarchy - 1 January 1527
- Creation of Yugoslavia - 4 December 1918
- Declaration of independence - 25 June 1991

International rankings:
No. 62 in the Worldwide Press Freedom Index
No. 82 in the Index of Economic Freedom
No. 62 in the International Corruption Perceptions Index
No. 45 in the Human Development Index

Croatia	Value
% of world GDP, 2018	0.06
% of world exports, 2018	0.13
% of world imports, 2018	0.13
% of world Foreign Direct Investment, 2018	0.12
Innovations index (0-100), 2021	37.3
R & D expenditure, % of GDP, 2018	0.97

Information technology exports, % of total goods exports, 2019	2.33
High technology exports, $ million, 2020	1.10
Patent applications by residents, 2019	195
Wind electricity generation, billion kilowatthours, 2020	1.72
Solar electricity generation, billion kilowatthours, 2020	0.1
Hydroelectricity generation, billion kilowatthours, 2020	5.87
Renewable power generation, billion kilowatthours, 2020	9.7
Quality of air transport infrastructure, 1(low) - 7(high), 2019	4.80
Airline passengers of domestically owned airlines, mln, 2019	2.11

Czechia

Economic growth: 2.3% (2022)
Exports/Imports ($bln): 161/140

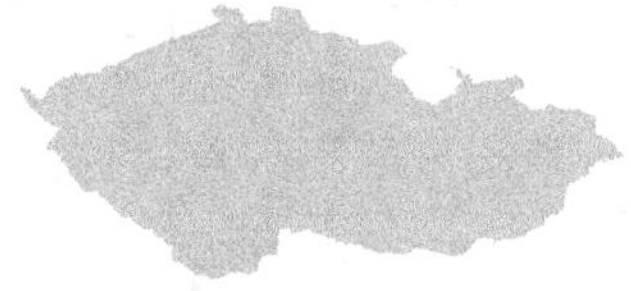

Main dates from history:
- Duchy of Bohemia - 870
- Kingdom of Bohemia - 1198
- Czechoslovakia - 28 October 1918
- Czech Republic - 1 January 1993

International rankings:
No. 7 in the Global Peace Index
No. 28 in the Human Development Index
No. 24 in the Index of Economic Freedom
No. 34 in the Reporters Without Borders worldwide Press Freedom Index
No. 39 in the World Economic Forum Travel & Tourism Competitiveness Report

Czechia	Value
% of world GDP, 2018	0.25
% of world exports, 2018	0.78
% of world imports, 2018	0.73
% of world Foreign Direct Investment, 2018	0.81
Innovations index (0-100), 2021	49
R & D expenditure, % of GDP, 2018	1.93
Information technology exports, % of total goods exports, 2019	16.17
High technology exports, $ million, 2020	39.60

Patent applications by residents, 2019	765
Wind electricity generation, billion kilowatthours, 2020	0.7
Solar electricity generation, billion kilowatthours, 2020	2.24
Hydroelectricity generation, billion kilowatthours, 2020	2.15
Renewable power generation, billion kilowatthours, 2020	9.9
Quality of air transport infrastructure, 1(low) - 7(high), 2019	5.00
Airline passengers of domestically owned airlines, mln, 2019	5.45

Estonia

Economic growth: 1.6% (2022)
Exports/Imports ($bln): 14/16

Main dates from history:
- Declaration of independence - 24 February 1918
- German occupation - February–November 1918
- Power handover to national government - 11–14 November 1918
- Soviet invasion and occupation - 1940–1941
- German occupation - 1941–1944
- Soviet occupation - 1944–1991
- Independence restored - 20 August 1991

International rankings:
No. 36 in the Global Peace Index – Institute for Economics and Peace
No. 64 in the CIA World Factbook – GDP per capita (PPP)
No. 85 in the CIA World Factbook – life expectancy
No. 14 in the World Economic Forum – Enabling Trade Index ranking
No. 8 in the Yale University – Environmental Performance Index

Estonia	Value
% of world GDP, 2018	0.03
% of world exports, 2018	0.09
% of world imports, 2018	0.09
% of world Foreign Direct Investment, 2018	0.12
Innovations index (0-100), 2021	49.9
R & D expenditure, % of GDP, 2018	1.43

Information technology exports, % of total goods exports, 2019	7.59
High technology exports, $ million, 2020	2.20
Patent applications by residents, 2019	31
Wind electricity generation, billion kilowatthours, 2020	0.84
Solar electricity generation, billion kilowatthours, 2020	0.12
Hydroelectricity generation, billion kilowatthours, 2020	0.04
Renewable power generation, billion kilowatthours, 2020	1.77
Quality of air transport infrastructure, 1(low) - 7(high), 2019	4.60
Airline passengers of domestically owned airlines, mln, 2019	0

Hungary

Economic growth: 4.0% (2022)
Exports/Imports ($bln): 126/116

Main dates from history:

- Principality of Hungary - 895
- Christian Kingdom - 25 December 1000
- Battle of Mohács - 29 August 1526
- Liberation of Buda - 2 September 1686
- Revolution of 1848 - 15 March 1848
- Third Republic - 23 October 1989

International rankings:

No. 1 in the Consumption tax / VAT
No. 54 in the Index of Economic Freedom
No. 41 in the Ease of Doing Business Index
No. 28 in the Inequality adjusted Human Development Index
No. 20 in the Trade Freedom Index

Hungary	Value
% of world GDP, 2018	0.16
% of world exports, 2018	0.55
% of world imports, 2018	0.53
% of world Foreign Direct Investment, 2018	-6.31

Innovations index (0-100), 2021	42.7
R & D expenditure, % of GDP, 2018	1.55
Information technology exports, % of total goods exports, 2019	12.82
High technology exports, $ million, 2020	18.10
Patent applications by residents, 2019	427
Wind electricity generation, billion kilowatthours, 2020	0.66
Solar electricity generation, billion kilowatthours, 2020	2.45
Hydroelectricity generation, billion kilowatthours, 2020	0.24
Renewable power generation, billion kilowatthours, 2020	5.6
Quality of air transport infrastructure, 1(low) - 7(high), 2019	4.60
Airline passengers of domestically owned airlines, mln, 2019	39.8

Latvia

Economic growth: 3.9% (2022)
Exports/Imports ($bln): 13/16

Main dates from history:
- Declaration of independence - 18 November 1918
- Recognised - 26 January 1921
- Constitution - 7 November 1922
- Restored after Soviet occupation - 21 August 1991
- Joined the EU - 1 May 2004

International rankings:
No. 13 in the Sustainable Society Index Economic Wellbeing
No. 19 in the Ease of doing business index 2019
No. 35 in the Index of Economic Freedom
No. 24 in the Economic Freedom of the World
No. 3 in the International Tax Competitiveness Index

Latvia	Value
% of world GDP, 2018	0.03
% of world exports, 2018	0.09
% of world imports, 2018	0.09
% of world Foreign Direct Investment, 2018	0.04
Innovations index (0-100), 2021	40
R & D expenditure, % of GDP, 2018	0.63
Information technology exports, % of total goods exports, 2019	8.94
High technology exports, $ million, 2020	1.80

Patent applications by residents, 2019	82
Wind electricity generation, billion kilowatthours, 2020	0.18
Solar electricity generation, billion kilowatthours, 2020	0.01
Hydroelectricity generation, billion kilowatthours, 2020	2.57
Renewable power generation, billion kilowatthours, 2020	3.55
Quality of air transport infrastructure, 1(low) - 7(high), 2019	5.70
Airline passengers of domestically owned airlines, mln, 2019	4.98

Lithuania

Economic growth: 1.9% (2022)
Exports/Imports ($bln): 29/32

Main dates from history:
- Grand Duchy - 1236
- Coronation of Mindaugas - 6 July 1253
- Union with Poland - 2 February 1386
- Polish-Lithuanian Commonwealth - 1 July 1569
- Partitioned - 24 October 1795
- Independence reinstated - 16 February 1918
- Independence restored - 11 March 1990

International rankings:
No. 34 in the Human Development Index
No. 36 in the Global Peace Index
No. 4 in the Transformation Index BTI
No. 34 in the Legatum Prosperity Index
No. 11 in the Ease of Doing Business Index

Lithuania	Value
% of world GDP, 2018	0.05
% of world exports, 2018	0.16
% of world imports, 2018	0.16
% of world Foreign Direct Investment, 2018	0.13
Innovations index (0-100), 2021	39.9
R & D expenditure, % of GDP, 2018	0.94
Information technology exports, % of total goods exports, 2019	3.44
High technology exports, $ million, 2020	2.60
Patent applications by residents, 2019	90
Wind electricity generation, billion kilowatthours, 2020	1.55
Solar electricity generation, billion kilowatthours, 2020	0.13
Hydroelectricity generation, billion kilowatthours, 2020	0.39
Renewable power generation, billion kilowatthours, 2020	2.62
Quality of air transport infrastructure, 1(low) - 7(high), 2019	4.90
Airline passengers of domestically owned airlines, mln, 2019	0

Poland

Economic growth: 4.8% (2022)
Exports/Imports ($bln): 230/228

Main dates from history:
• Baptism of Poland - 14 April 966
• Kingdom of Poland - 18 April 1025
• Polish–Lithuanian Commonwealth - 1 July 1569
• Partitions of Poland - 24 October 1795
• Second Republic - 11 November 1918
• People's Republic - 19 February 1947

• Third Republic - 31 December 1989

International rankings:
No. 10 in the EF English Proficiency Index
No. 34 in the Education Index
No. 39 in the Global Innovation Index
No. 42 in the Index of Economic Freedom
No. 24 in the World Bank Group Ease of Doing Business

Interesting facts:
- Poland is named after an ancient Slavic Tribe (Polanie)
- It is the most religious country in Europe (90% Catholics).
- Poland is the biggest exporter of Amber in the world.
- 35% of Poland are forests
- Country has 40 R&D centres

Between 1989 and 2018, Poland's GDP increased by 827% (the highest growth in Europe), in a comparison in the same period to Ireland's GDP growth by 789%, Slovakia's by 784% and the Czech Republic by 549%. In 1990, the Polish national income amounted to $65.978 billion, and by 2021 it had increased to $655 billion nominal. Achieving these results was possible thanks to the privatization of state-owned firms, the development of private entrepreneurship, the rapid increase in work efficiency and foreign direct investments. The Polish economy grew by 5.4% (2018) 4.5% (2019), −2.8% (2020), and 5.4% (2021).
GDP by sector: agriculture: 2.4%, industry: 40.2%, services: 57.4%. Inflation: 2.3%. Unemployment: 3.1%. Average net salary per month: $1.153.

Foreign trade and FDI

With the collapse of the Soviet empire in 1991, Poland reoriented its trade from Eastern Europe to Western Europe and now over 70% of its trade overall is with EU members.
Poland's Exports - $230 billion (2020),
Poland's Imports - $228 billion (2020),

Poland's main trading partner today are:
- In exports: Germany, Czechia, United Kingdom and France
- In imports: Germany, China, Russia and Netherlands
Among the 3SI countries:
- In exports: Czech Republic, Hungary, Slovakia, and Austria
- In imports: Czech Republic, Hungary, Slovakia, and Austria

Before Joining the EU, Poland fostered regional integration and trade through the Central European Free Trade Agreement (CEFTA), which included Hungary, the Czech Republic, Slovakia and Slovenia.
Poland is a founding member of the World Trade Organization (WTO), and a member of OECD.
Poland's major imports are machinery and transport equipment 38%, intermediate manufactured goods 21%, chemicals 15%, minerals, fuels, lubricants and related materials 9%.
The most successful exports are furniture, foods, motor boats, light planes, hardwood products, casual clothing, shoes and cosmetics.
Poland ranks in the top 20 in the world both in terms of exports and imports, recording a clear trade surplus.
Foreign Direct Investment (FDI), as % of GDP, 2019: 2.42

Trade balance, % of GDP, 2020: 6.76

Poland	Value
% of world GDP, 2018	0.6
% of world exports, 2018	1.32
% of world imports, 2018	1.27
% of world Foreign Direct Investment, 2018	1.72
Innovations index (0-100), 2021	39.9
R & D expenditure, % of GDP, 2018	1.21
Information technology exports, % of total goods exports, 2019	6.55
High technology exports, $ million, 2020	20.30
Patent applications by residents, 2019	3.887
Wind electricity generation, billion kilowatthours, 2020	15.8
Solar electricity generation, billion kilowatthours, 2020	1.99
Hydroelectricity generation, billion kilowatthours, 2020	2.15
Renewable power generation, billion kilowatthours, 2020	27.66
Quality of air transport infrastructure, 1(low) - 7(high), 2019	4.80
Airline passengers of domestically owned airlines, mln, 2019	10.23

Romania

Economic growth: 3.9% (2022)
Exports/Imports ($bln): 85/88

International rankings (in the world):
No. 30 in the GDP per capita growth (4.56%)
No. 34 in the Income Tax Rate (16%)
No. 23 in the Tax Burden Index (90.3)
No. 32 in the Foreign direct investment net inflows ($7.3 billion)
No. 41 in the Total reserves including gold ($42.1 billion)

Main dates from history:
• Unification - 24 January 1859
• Independence - 9 May 1878
• Greater Romania - 1918
• Socialist Republic - 30 December 1947
• Current Republic - 27 December 1989

Interesting facts:
- The name "Romania" comes from the Latin word "Romanus" which means "citizen of the Roman Empire."
- The Romanian language is 1.700 years old
- The Parliament Palace in Bucharest is the second largest building in the world (behind the Pentagon).
- Stefan Odobleja laid the foundations of Cybernetics in1941.
- Romania is famous for its medieval castles in Transylvania

Romania	Value

% of world GDP, 2018	0.24
% of world exports, 2018	0.41
% of world imports, 2018	0.45
% of world Foreign Direct Investment, 2018	0.72
Innovations index (0-100), 2021	35.6
R & D expenditure, % of GDP, 2018	0.51
Information technology exports, % of total goods exports, 2019	3.2
High technology exports, $ million, 2020	7.00
Patent applications by residents, 2019	881
Wind electricity generation, billion kilowatthours, 2020	6.95
Solar electricity generation, billion kilowatthours, 2020	1.77
Hydroelectricity generation, billion kilowatthours, 2020	15.65
Renewable power generation, billion kilowatthours, 2020	24.67
Quality of air transport infrastructure, 1(low) - 7(high), 2019	4.60
Airline passengers of domestically owned airlines, mln, 2019	5.63

Slovakia

Economic growth: 2.3% (2022)
Exports/Imports ($bln): 81/80

Main dates from history:
• Independence (First Czechoslovak Republic) - 28 October 1918
• Third Czechoslovak Republic - 24 October 1945
• Czechoslovak Socialist Republic - 11 July 1960
• Slovak Republic - 1 March 1990
• Current Republic - 1 January 1993

International rankings:
No. 38 in the Human Development Index
No. 57 in the Index of Economic Freedom 2017
No. 41 in the Global Competitiveness Report
No. 57 in the Corruption Perceptions Index
No. 22 in the Global Peace Index

Slovakia	Value
% of world GDP, 2018	0.11
% of world exports, 2018	0.41
% of world imports, 2018	0.41
% of world Foreign Direct Investment, 2018	0.22
Innovations index (0-100), 2021	40.2
R & D expenditure, % of GDP, 2018	0.83

Information technology exports, % of total goods exports, 2019	13.28
High technology exports, $ million, 2020	8.00
Patent applications by residents, 2019	206
Wind electricity generation, billion kilowatthours, 2020	0.01
Solar electricity generation, billion kilowatthours, 2020	0.66
Hydroelectricity generation, billion kilowatthours, 2020	4.47
Renewable power generation, billion kilowatthours, 2020	6.69
Quality of air transport infrastructure, 1(low) - 7(high), 2019	3.80
Airline passengers of domestically owned airlines, mln, 2019	0

Slovenia

Economic growth: 5.4% (2022)
Exports/Imports ($bln): 33/32

Main dates from history:
- State of Slovenes, Croats and Serbs - 29 October 1918
- Slovene National Liberation Committee - 19 February 1944
- Socialist Federal Republic of Yugoslavia - 29 July 1944
- Independence from Yugoslavia - 25 June 1991
- Current constitution - 23 December 1991

International rankings:
No. 61 in the Index of Economic Freedom
No. 27 in the Corruption Perceptions Index
No. 29 in the Human Development Index
No. 11 in the Institute for Economics and Peace Global Peace Index
No. 5 in the Privacy index

Slovenia	Value
% of world GDP, 2018	0.05
% of world exports, 2018	0.19
% of world imports, 2018	0.17
% of world Foreign Direct Investment, 2018	0.15
Innovations index (0-100), 2021	44.1
R & D expenditure, % of GDP, 2018	1.94
Information technology exports, % of total goods exports, 2019	1.79
High technology exports, $ million, 2020	2.50

Patent applications by residents, 2019	255
Wind electricity generation, billion kilowatthours, 2020	0.01
Solar electricity generation, billion kilowatthours, 2020	0.37
Hydroelectricity generation, billion kilowatthours, 2020	5.02
Renewable power generation, billion kilowatthours, 2020	5.6
Quality of air transport infrastructure, 1(low) - 7(high), 2019	4.60
Airline passengers of domestically owned airlines, mln, 2019	0.87

Chapter 4 – Digital 3SI

Digital economy is defined as an economy that focuses on digital technologies. It essentially covers all kind of activities that are supported by the internet and other digital communication technologies.

The biggest digital economies in the world are the USA, China, Germany, Japan, and the UK, but also the 3SI countries created impressive, and fast pace digital sectors. Polish digital economy grew by 7.2 % in 2019, reaching a value of $32.7 billion, Austria was ranked 10th in Digital Economy and Society Index (DESI 2017), and according to McKinsey the Czech digital economy accounted for 7.8% of the nation's GDP and grew at triple the speed of the rest of the economy.

High technology exports in the 3SI countries combined reached a value of $120 billion in 2020 (Germany $181 billion, South Korea $164 billion). Romania according to DAXX, with an estimated 100.000 software engineers, is among the countries with the highest number of software developers in the world (Singapore – 200.000, Mexico – 100.000). Considering R & D expenditure as % of GDP (2018), Austria reached 3.17%, Slovenia 1.94%, and Czechia 1.93% in comparison to the world leaders: Israel – 4.95%, and South Korea – 4.91%.

Thomas Mesenbourg mentions three components of digital economy, namely infrastructure, e-business, and e-commerce. The 3SI countries are very competitive in all of them, however they need capital from countries such as the US, UK, and Japan. Specialists from Central Europe often emigrate as they cannot develop, working in small and medium size firms that lacking resources for further expansion. The 3SI states' universities are able to supply quality experts in Artificial Intelligence, Quantum communication, Quantum calculations, Bioengineering, Biotechnology, Space technologies, Material engineering. Digital transformation in the region has enormous speed adopting new technologies to change services and businesses. Manual (non-digital) processes are replace by digital ones or replacing outdated digital technology with upgraded digital technology.

The rapid adoption of new digital technology is changing everyday life. But digitisation does not seem to have boosted productivity, the elixir of economic growth. This does not necessarily make it less relevant than the headlines make out. History shows the practical benefits of ground-breaking technologies take time to show up. But it does underline the need for high-speed broadband networks and supporting investments, notably in human capital, if companies are to make the most of artificial intelligence and other innovations. And a firm grasp of the driving forces of productivity and the adoption of new technologies at the firm level will be critical to the formulation of effective public policies to realise the potential of the digital economy.[3]

The 3SI offers great opportunities in digital infrastructure projects that will boost economic growth, innovation and competitiveness in the region. Except the capital, know-how is most welcome to exchange of knowledge and good practices in the areas of digitalisation in education, healthcare, public administration and business.

---

[3] www.frontier-economics.com/uk/en/news-and-articles/articles/article-i6483-competitiveness-and-the-digital-economy/

Chapter 5 – Energy 3SI

In the 3SI, and other European Union countries last a big transformation from the traditional energy to renewable energy, that is also called 'clean energy', and is energy collected from natural resources such as sunlight, wind, rain, tides, waves, and geothermal heat.

Nuclear-generated electricity isn't renewable but it's zero-carbon, which means its generation emits low levels or almost no CO2, just like renewable energy sources. A big advantage of nuclear energy is a fact that it's not dependent on the weather. Natural gas may also seem to be renewable source of energy but it is not. Central European governments want gas to be treated as a temporary solution in their shift to renewable energy only economy, which will take many years before it will actually happen. There is a chance that the European Union will follow their suggestions, especially now, in the times of Russian aggression on Ukraine. The 3SI states are planning to increase investments in LNG, and gas infrastructure as well as new nuclear reactors. The US - their powerful ally from NATO – became a leading nation in the production of gas. The United States was number 3 in the world in terms of Liquefied Natural Gas (LNG) exports in 2021 after Australia and Qatar. These three countries accounted for 60% of global LNG exports. The USA sold 70.43 million tonnes (compare to 47.35 million tonnes in 2020), including 24.07 million tons to Europe, and will increase its production and exports in the following years. Central Europe will be a main destination of the US LNG.

Traditional energy is also called 'dirty energy', and its source comes from three fossil fuels: coal, oil, and natural gas. Up until now these fuels were the cheapest way to produce energy not only in the 3SI countries. For example,

Poland is a leading nation in terms of production, export and import of coal. The country is the 5th biggest exporter of coal in the world (5.2 million tons in 2020). Czechia is no. 8 in the world (1.5 million tons).

Poland is also no. 6 among biggest importers of coal in the world (14.4 million tons in 2020). Czechia is the 15th biggest importer in the world (almost 4 million tons), Austria is no. 17th (3.3 million tons), followed by Slovakia (3.2 million tons).

In terms of coal consumption Poland is no. 4 in the world (120 million tons), Czechia is no. 7 in the world (38.8 million tons).

Production of coal in Poland (110.6 million tons in 2020) set the country as no. 3 in the world. Czechia is no. 7 among biggest producers (34.8 million tons), Hungary no. 10 (6.8 million tons), Slovenia no. 11 (3.5 million tons), and Slovakia no. 15 (1.1 million tons).

Being rich in "unclean" sources of energy Central Europe has not easy task to transform its economies in such a way to use only environment friendly energy. The 3SI can be a good platform to do it together. That would reduce huge costs of that transformation, and diminish time scope for the whole process.

Chapter 6 – Transport 3SI

For 3SI countries' economies efficient transport is essential to bring together the inputs used in the production of goods and services and getting outputs from the production process to customers. Modes of transport include air, rail, road, water, and even space. Central Europe has been invested a lot in the networks of transport, especially in motorways in recent decades, because they connect west with east, and north with south. For example, the air transport is an important enabler to achieving economic growth in Central Europe helping integrate the region with the global economy and provides dynamic connectivity on a national, regional, and international scale. One of the Polish government infrastructural projects is to build from scratch the Central Communication Port (Centralny Port Komunikacyjny, CPK), 40 kilometres southwest of Warsaw. It is an airport that is aim to replace by 2027 Chopin Airport in Warsaw, which is gradually getting surrounded by rapidly expanding city. The combined airport and train station will plan to serve 40 million passengers per year (same as Berlin Brandenburg Airport - and grow to capacity of 100 million passengers. Planned train connections will take 15 minutes to Warsaw Central station, 2 hours to most major Polish cities, and a high-speed train to German Frankfurt (Oder), which is to shorten the travel time on the Berlin - Warsaw route. The expected costs of the investment are estimated between $10 billion and $20 billion including the airport, high-speed railways and motorways. According to Prime Minister Morawiecki this investment is a major logistic solution for the 3SI countries, and will open it for new investors, tourists, and employees.

In terms of motorways length the 3SI countries had in 2021 over 14.000 km of motorways in total (Poland 4.368 km, Austria 1.743 km, Hungary 1.600 km, Croatia 1.310 km, Czechia 1.306 km). This shows a fantastic progress made in the last two decades in Central Europe. To compare to western countries: Germany has 13.183 km of motorways, France 11.671 km, Spain 17.228 km, Italy 6.943 km. Poland has a longer networks of motorways than the UK and Portugal. Austria and Hungary have a longer motorway networks than Russia.

In terms of railways length the 3SI countries had in 2019 over 66.447 km of railways including Poland 18.538 km, Romania 10.759 km, Czechia 9.396 km, and Hungary 7.588 km. To compare to western countries: Germany 39.379 km, France 27.483 km. Poland has a longer rail network than the UK and Italy, Romania have a longer railway network than Finland and Switzerland.

The 3SI can be a great platform for programmes and projects to expand and connect transport networks in the region. There is an urgent need for high speed railways infrastructure, and for new canals that would connect main rivers in Central Europe enabling new trade routes. Some 3SI countries have own space agencies, and space industry that began participation in the space exploration. New created Low Earth Orbit economy will have a great impact on the twelve Central European states in the near future.

PART 2 - The 3SI – US & UK Engagement

Chapter 1 - 3SI – US Engagement

Why the USA should be engaged in the 3SI?

Why the USA should be engaged in the 3SI? Because Washington has ambition to maintain his position as the world leader, super power, and a hegemon that decides about the most important processes shaping the globe. The 3SI countries rely on the US as the main guarantor of their independence, and see its strategic engagement in the region as a necessary condition of prosperity in Central Europe.

The US are three times bigger than the 3SI countries combined, they also have three times bigger population, and eleven times bigger economy. The USA sent in 2020 goods and services to the 3SI countries for $17.3 billion, and imported from the 3SI for $45 billion.[4] These was less than one percent of all its exports, very little to maintain a strong relationship with the region.

Schmitt & Larot

To better understand importance of the 3SI for the USA as a world hegemon it is necessary to refer to geopolitics, geostrategy, and geo-economics. Carl Schmitt (1888-1985) – a German intellectualist - created own geopolitical concept that the "key" to recognising the mechanism of history is the conflict between the "maritime" and "land" powers, with the legendary "Leviathan" being the personification of the sea power, and the land power - "Behemoth". As an argument for

---

[4] tradingeconomics.com

that he gives examples from the past: rivalry between Athens and Sparta, Cartage and Rome, UK and France, the USA and the Soviet Union, and now between the USA (a maritime power), and China (a land power). Following this idea, Washington should use its influence in the region to stop growing Chinese domination in Eurasia, blocking the New Silk Road, otherwise it may lose its hegemony in Europe and in the world.

According to geo-economists such as Luttwak and Larot, military power is replaced by economic ability and power in the contemporary world. Economic development was the key reason why USA and China became super powers, not military conquests. These days even small and mid-size countries can become economic powerhouses (Singapore, South Korea). Economic development also is the main factor determining the classification of the 3SI countries on the international stage. It is actually odd that the United States concentrated so much on cooperation with Pakistan and Israel, and much less on collaboration with the 3SI – the fasted growing economies in the world.

Central Europeans in the USA
According to "2016 American Community Survey – People Reporting Ancestry" big diasporas of the 3SI nations live in the US: Polish – 9.3 millions, Czechs - 1.4 millions, Hungarians – 1.4 millions, Slovaks – 0.7 million, Austrians – 0.7 million, Lithuanians – 0.6 million, Romanians – 0.5 million, Croatians – 0.4 million. It is important to know that in total, there is around 16 millions of American citizens (out of 319 millions). 5% of the American population recognise that their parents, or grandparents came from the 3SI nations, and have positive feelings about their relations with countries such as Romania or Slovakia. This fact can be used to promote bigger

collaboration between the US and 3SI, influence at candidates on American elections, and support democratic changes in Washington profitable for the 3SI countries. Sixteen million potential voters are able to introduce own congressmen and senators if the 3SI nations learn how to cooperate on the American soil.

USA vs China

Rivalry between USA and China is visible in all parts of the world including the 3SI states. In 2020 the USA exported to the region four times less than China ($17 billion vs $70 billion), imported more goods and services than China ($45 billion vs 32 billion).

The U.S. investments made in Europe were valued at $3.66 trillion (out of $6.15 trillion in the world).

Portalstatystyczny.pl wrote that meanwhile by 2021 the US firms invested in Poland $24.4 billion, and employed 267.000 people. That was only 11% of all foreign investments, and only 4% of Polish GDP. 1500 American firms in Poland are important part of economy, but these figures clearly show that the US economic engagement in Poland and other 3SI nations is really minimal, and China does not need to do much afford in the region to exceed American involvement.

The US Decoupling[5] from China and onshoring[6] of critical supply chains, which started with the covid pandemic, creates new opportunities for US engagement in the 3SI countries. The serious supply chain vulnerabilities that have been exposed in recent years, made an important shift in US policy and regulations towards China to better protect US

---

[5] **Decoupling** - Decoupling refer to a disconnect between a country's investment market performance and the state of its underlying economy.
[6] **Onshoring** - refers to the overall practice of moving manufacturing operations from foreign soil back to home country.

technologies, intellectual property and data, and to end US dependence on China for strategically important materials, components, and products. The 3SI countries are great place to move (onshore) some of the American businesses from China to Europe, reducing the United States' reliance on fragile supply chains insulating the US economy from future disruptions like those seen over the last two years.

In 2020, the U.S. investments made in China have been growing constantly valued at $123.9 billion ($114 billion in 2019, $108 billion in 2018, and $105 billion in 2017), despite increasing tensions between China and the US. Washington should be able to onshore some of its factories (at least 20%) to the USA in the near future after re-calculating all costs and benefits, and around ten percent of them should be suitable to find their home in the US European allies such as Czechia or Poland. Without decoupling and onshoring America will lose its hegemony in the world in next two decades, loosing also its influence in Europe. The US investments in the 3SI countries (over $60 billion so far) which is a surprisingly small engagement in comparison to the US engagement in Pakistan ($78 billion between 1946-2016), Israel ($146 billion since the second war), and Taiwan ($31.5 billion direct investments only in 2020).

USA vs Germany

Comparing US engagement in the 3SI with the German one shows who is the real hegemon in Central Europe: the US export 15 times less ($17 billion vs $269 billion), and import 5 times less than the Germans ($45 billion vs $243 billion). Obviously Germany is close, and has the European Union with its funds but there should not be such a huge chasm between these two powers. After leaving the EU by the United Kingdom the Americans are even more needed because two visions of Europe are at stack: a European federation and a confederation of independent countries. The 3SI countries - who experienced tyrannies of empires in the past -are eager to choose the second option, doing everything to save its sovereignty that has been more and more limited by Brussels. The Union of independent states is also a better option for Washington who does not need a European superpower run by Germany to compete with.

USA vs Russia

Comparing the US engagement in the 3SI with the Russian one we can see that the Americans export less goods and services ($17 billion vs $33 billion), and import more from the 3SI than the Russians ($45 billion vs $19 billion). Even Russia with its messy economy could increase trade with the region several times if there is a political will on Kremlin. Moscow has a great opportunity to show its advantage over Washington in trade with the 3SI states.

Digital

Considering the US engagement in the Digital 3SI it's necessary to mention about Google and Microsoft $3 billion investment programmes in Poland. These are not 3SI projects but they show how good for the region can be a technological impact from the US. In 2020 Google started building Google Cloud, and Microsoft its regional technology hub with the Polish National Cloud - the company's first data processing region in Central and Eastern Europe. Both projects are to significantly boost the domestic economy and make Poland one of the main digital hubs in Europe.

After launching the Google Cloud region in Poland, Google focused on another cloud investment: a Technology Development Center in Warsaw. It is the largest center in

Europe employing experts in cloud computing technology, who work on the key components of Google Cloud technology, services that dynamically allocate computing power to data centers for business customers, virtual machines, as well as for the proper operation of the global network connecting Google cloud services, and developing the most advanced solutions, and products for cloud computing.

These major high-tech firms investments attracted many other technological corporations, e.g. British Endava.

Digital 3SI is also an excellent area for bigger US engagement. All 3SI countries except Austria are part of the NATO, that rely on strong and resilient cyber defences to fulfil the Alliance's core tasks of collective defence, crisis management and cooperative security. NATO's main focus in cyber defence is to protect its own networks (including operations and missions) and enhance resilience across the Alliance. The US lead in all four cybersecurity domains: the physical one (hardware and software); the information domain (confidentiality, integrity and availability of information); the cognitive one (how information is perceived and analysed); and the social domain (attention to ethics, and social norms). Possible future US investments in the digital 3SI could support not only military and governments' cyberspace but also economic infrastructure. Strong cybersecurity is essential for the companies which are national champions in Central Europe (e.g. ORLEN, MOL, OVM), which are part of the critical national infrastructure of their home countries. This makes it a high-value target for potential cyber attackers.

Digital 3SI could work with the Americans on projects to improve coordination between cyberwarfare forces such as Cyber Command in Estonia, and Cybernetic Operations Center in Poland.

Transport

The US engagement in the 3SI transport would improve routes for NATO forces, which need to be quickly deploy in a situation of security threats for American allies in Central Europe. The region has more than enough airbases and airports that were built during the Cold Wars, but they need to be modernised and adjust to strategic plans of Washington (NATO), e.g. how many troops the US want to deploy, and in which country as a response to a potential threat? For example, the east-west and north-south transport routes leading through Poland, can be used by NATO military units in Europe, and are necessary for the effective implementation of the defence discouragement policy. Strengthening military mobility on the eastern border of NATO is an important factor for the efficient deployment of troops in the event of a potential conflict with Russia.

Energy

Energy as a sector of economy became more important than ever, because it is integral part of national security for majority countries in the world. A healthy economy must have diverse energy supplies, balance between home and external energy sources, and move swiftly from traditional to renewable energy.

All twelve 3SI economies still heavily depend on Russian oil and gas supplies, in spite of over thirty years of economic transformation.

Fortunately for the 3SI a technological progress in extracting oil and gas made in recent years, reduced the costs, and made the USA a major Liquefied Natural Gas (LNG) exporter. First LNG was delivered in 1964 but only in the last decade the costs of production and transport were reduced to such a low level, that it is profitable for firms to ship it from remote parts of the world. LNG is a clear, colourless and non-toxic liquid which forms when natural gas is cooled to -162ºC. The cooling process shrinks the volume of the gas 600 times, making it easier and safer to store and ship. In its liquid state, LNG will not ignite. When LNG reaches its destination, it is turned back into a gas at regasification plants. It is then piped to homes, businesses and industries where it is burnt for heat or to generate electricity. LNG is now also emerging as a cost-competitive and cleaner transport fuel, especially for shipping and heavy-duty road transport.

In 2021 three countries exported 60% of all LNG gas: Australia (80.2 million tons), Qatar (77.8 million tons), and the USA (70.4 million tons). The US significantly increased its export from 47.4 million tons in 2020, and planning to export much more in the following years, selling it to the 3SI countries too. In the same year Poland imported 3.76 billion m³ (including 1.04 billion m³ from the US), and signing new contracts for more LNG gas. Liquefied gas will not replace natural gas in the near future but it can increase the 3SI countries' energy independence. Therefore Central Europe builds new LNG terminals, gas pipelines and connectors, counting on the US support in energy sector.

Issues with Nord Stream 2 will be remembered for a long time in Europe. President Trump opposed of building that gas pipeline from Russia to Germany, supporting Central Europe states' claims that it could be used as a blackmail tool, but president Biden decided to accept the German point of view that it is fully commercial project. It was a great disappointment for the region, especially when in August 2021 the American officials arrived to Kiev and Warsaw suggesting that Poland and Ukraine should stop criticising the US deal with Germany allowing to finish the Nord Stream, otherwise their relationships with American may be worsen. This considerably damaged the US reputation in the region.

According to Shell Corp. global LNG demand will grow to 700 million tonnes by 2040 (360 million in 2020), which shows that it cannot be alternative for Russian gas in the near future but can be an important part of energy diversification for the 3SI states.

LNG is the cleanest fossil fuel. In the context of the current energy transition sought by the European Union, it represents an excellent alternative to reduce greenhouse gas emissions in contrary to shale gas.

Shale gas

Shale gas has the same composition as natural gas, the difference between the types of gases are the locations of the reservoirs. Natural gas can be found in big amounts, while shale gas is trapped inside the microcracks of a rock. The 3SI countries don't have much natural gas and have to import it, e.g. from Russia. However, Central Europe is rich in shale gas! Shale-gas discoveries are also opening up substantial new resources of tight oil, also known as shale oil.

Shale gas has become an increasingly important source of natural gas in the USA: In 2000 it provided only 1% of U.S. natural gas production; by 2010 it was 20% and is expected that 46% of the United States' natural gas supply will come from shale gas by 2035.

The estimates from 2020 indicate that recoverable gas resources from shale formations are between 190 and 260 billion cubic meters in Central Europe, but there must be much more than that. To compare, there are 90 billion cubic meters of natural gas resources in Poland that can be extracted.

Nuclear plants

Nuclear plants construction is a sector of economy where Washington can participate with its know-how, technology, and firms. The United States has 94 operating commercial nuclear reactors at 56 nuclear power plants in 28 states. The 3SI countries have: in operation: Bulgaria 2 nuclear reactors, Czechia 6, Hungary 4, Romania 2, Slovakia 4, Slovenia 1; under construction: Slovakia 2.7 Many European governments are planning to build them (Romania, Czechia, Poland) because a very strict EU regime regarding climate protection, force them to look for more environment friendly alternatives for coal plants that need to be closed soon. It is a huge chance for the US to strengthen it is position in the region, and gain new markets for American firms. Japan, South Korea, and France have already offered their involvement (e.g. in Poland), and Russia in Hungary. Most interested in investing in the region among American corporations is Westinghouse Electric Company that is a subsidiary of Toshiba, and offers nuclear fuel, services, technology, plant design and equipment. Another very competent firm is GE Hitachi Nuclear Energy, a partnership of General Electric and Hitachi (in Japan the partnership is Hitachi-GE Nuclear Energy), that is a provider of advanced reactor technology and nuclear services, including manufacturing nuclear fuel and uranium enrichment services. The cost of building 1.000 MW in nuclear power plants in Europe is approximately $10 billion. The 3SI countries will build at least 10 nuclear reactors in the next twenty years, so possible American investments in energy would exceed $100 billion. That would also increase national security in the region and transfer the latest technologies and know-how. One of the example of cooperation in the nuclear energy

---

[7] www.euronuclear.org/glossary/nuclear-power-plants-in-europe/

sector is the agreement from 2020 between the United States and Romania on the construction of two reactors at the Cernavoda nuclear power plant (the value of the project is $8 billion.

Another opportunity for the 3SI countries to modernised their energy sectors are small modular reactors (SNR). First SNR reactors will be built by 2030. The price and the ability to scale power by adding more reactors make SMR one of the most cost-effective methods of generating electricity. One reactor with a capacity of 300 MW is to cost about $1.2 billion. There are around 70 projects related to SMR reactors in the world now, and GE Hitachi is a leading company in terms of this revolutionary technology. It would be great if the 3SI countries focus on implementing SMR reactors in Central Europe.

Conclusion and perspectives

The main goal of the US engagement in the 3SI is to increase national security of the region, including energy security. Washington would gain a stable, friendly, and prosperous bloc of countries, that help Americans to anchor in Europe, controlling influence of Russia, China, and Germany. From the USA perspective Central Europe is a very important part of the world, but also very remote. The rivalry between US and China force Central Europe to choose between these two powers in many aspects of economy, security, and strategy. The New Silk Road may be attractive and profitable for countries such as Poland, but if Washington is against it, the US should be ready to offer better deals which compensate the 3SI states trade-offs.

	Total Export	Total Import 2020	USA to 3SI and 3SI to USA	
USA	$2.127 billion	$2.808 billion	$17 billion	0.8%

3SI	$977 billion	$966 billion	$45 billion	4.6%

	Area (km2)	Population	Nominal GDP, ($)	GDP (nominal, per capita)
USA	3.797.000	329.5 ml	22.9 tln	69.375
3SI	1.219.000	111.2 ml	2.1 tln	18.650

Main pros and cons for the 3SI states from their cooperation with the USA:

ADVANTAGES	DISADVANTAGES
Fast economic growth	National security depends on the very remote country
Increased national security	Conflict USA - China
Transfer of new technologies	
Increased security in energy	

Chapter 2 - 3SI – UK Engagement

Why the UK should be engaged in the 3SI?
Why the UK should be engaged in the 3SI? Because Great Britain wants to maintain its position of one of the richest and most influential countries in the world. To keep it the UK needs to strengthen its position in post Brexit Europe, through engagement in the project of the Three Seas in Central Europe. The first step was done in 2021 when two British minister took part in the 3SI summit in Sofia, Bulgaria.
The UK's exports of goods and services in 2020 totalled £601 billion and imports totalled £597 billion. The EU accounted for 42% of UK exports and 50% of UK imports. The largest trading partners of United Kingdom are USA, Germany, Netherlands, France and China. The 3SI countries export to the UK in 2020 equalled $36 billion, and imported from the United Kingdom equalled $18 billion. On a list of its largest trading partners based on data from Office for National Statistics (ONS) Poland is 15th, Czechia 24th, Austria 28th, and Hungary 32nd. It is very disappointing that the second most important ally of the 3SI countries has not been able to intensify its trade to the level of trade exchange between Germany and Central Europe. However, the combined trade between the 3SI countries and Britain equalled £40 billion ($54 billion), which would give the 3SI position number ten among trade partners, just behind Italy. Imports and exports have grown rapidly to and from Great Britain in recent years, and there is a chance that the 3SI states will be in the top 3 of trade partners in the near future.

Halford Mackinder

Considering the UK engagement in the 3SI it's necessary to mention English geographer Sir Halford Mackinder (1861-1947), academic and politician, one of the fathers of geopolitics and geostrategy, who created in 1902 his famous theory of the Heartland. He set out it in his essay: "The Geographical Pivot of History", that had a huge impact on social science in the XX century. Mackinder's reflections on the relationship between geography, history, and politics, was in line with the public debate on the relationship of Great Britain with European great powers before the World War. In that time, on the horizon of great politics, a new power appeared - the Second German Reich (1871-1914), whose main advantages were industrial power, demographic potential, technological innovation, decision-making capacity, land power and maritime potential. The combination of these factors threatened the Pax Britanica.

Mackinder lived in the atmosphere of fear of the collapse of the global order, trying to understand mechanisms that rule the world and decide about war and peace.

He claimed that continents are small islands in the universal ocean, and control of the land ensures control of the sea. The key to rule the world is the area of the Eurasian Great Steppe, which Mackinder calls the Heartland — belts of forests and steppes stretching from Poland, and Hungary to Mongolia.

According to the Mackinder's Geographical Axis of History, great politics consists of the following elements:

- Europe was created thanks to the presence and in opposition to the nomadic communities of the Great Steppe;

- On the one hand, the Old Continent consists of the "Atlantic" Romano-Germanic (sea) peoples, and on the other - the Slavic-Byzantine (land) peoples;

- In the modern (Colombian) era, when Atlantic Europe set out on the ocean, the Russian empire took the place and aspirations of nomads: land hunger, the search for natural borders, the militarist organization of the state, and the autocratic system;

- The threat to Europe at the beginning of the 20th century was a potential agreement between the great power (Russia) and the technocratic superpower (the Second German Reich);

- Geopolitics arose from the cause-and-effect relationships between geography and politics.[8]

Mackinder claimed that the strategic interests of the land powers and maritime powers intersect on so called Rimland (today's Three Seas Initiative countries), and the surrounding coastal waters. Control of these territories is crucial to stop the potential global hegemony of the intercontinental power.

Over a hundred years later, the United Kingdom is still main world power with similar challenges as it had before the First World War. The importance of Central Europe has not changed since that, and needs to be considered if the UK wants to stay a top power. Mackinder did not focus much on economy but it is obvious that contemporary geopolitics and geostrategy cannot exist without economy that influence them, and is influenced by them.

Central Europeans in the UK

According to the Office for National Statistics (ONS) the population of EU nationals in the UK dropped by 200.000 in 2020, from 3.7 million to 3.5 million. Around 5% of all the UK population are European nationals who dramatically improved catastrophic demographics of Great Britain, contributing billions of pounds to its economy.

Half of these Europeans who work and leave in the UK are citizens of 12 3SI citizens: Poland - 815.000, Romania –

---

[8] www.geopolityka.net/heartland-halforda-mackindera

404.000, Lithuania – 152.000, Bulgaria – 118.000, Hungary – 108.000, Latvia – 92.000, Slovakia – 77.000, Czechia – 36.000, Estonia – 13.000, Austria – 12.000, Croatia – 9.000, Slovenia – 5.000. According to the ONS data the vast majority of them keep their passports (around 90%), with only 7.000 a year applying for British citizenship. After Brexit it's expected that more the 3SI citizens would apply for it but the main issue is that those who did not apply for the British passports cannot vote during national elections. The British MPs are obviously more interested in the voice of own citizens. On the other hand, the 3SI countries who suffer demographic collapse have a bigger change to encourage them to come back home.

European Union estimated that over a million UK citizens lived and worked in the EU countries in 2020. One third of them enjoy sunshine in Spain but many British moved to the 3SI countries: Austria – 11.000, Czechia – 7.000, Hungary – 3.000, Bulgaria – 3.000, Romania – 2.000, Poland – 2.000, Slovakia – 2.000, Estonia – 1.000, Croatia, Slovenia, Lithuania, and Latvia – less than 1.000 each.

Onshoring of supply chains to UK and 3SI

According to United Nations Conference on Trade and Development the UK is the world vice leader (after the US) as an FDI destination, with the total inward FDI stock increasing from $2.1 trillion in 2019 to $2.2 trillion in 2020. It is also second most attractive (after Germany) country for investments from the 3SI countries. By individual country, the UK's highest overall investment was in the USA (£6.6 billion), followed by Ireland (£6.4 billion).

The British firms have invested so far almost $38 billion in Poland – around a quarter of all its investments in the 3SI countries. It is a great, significant involvement in the local economy but the UK could invest much more by moving /

onshoring some of its factories from China. That would strengthen the value chains in Britain, supporting job creation and levelling up in the UK. Not all types of projects will be profitable to onshore to the UK and then to 3SI countries after 2022 but majority of British exporters with factories in China should consider new chances which Central Europe give them as more attractive place for their businesses. Many British exporters sell products made in their Chinese factors for European customers losing money on very long supply chains in a situation they can produce the same goods in Europe, using the 3SI as a platform to invest in digital, transport and energy, reopening trade with Europe.

This would also increase the number of jobs in the UK. Assessing distributional implications will require an understanding of supported sector supply chains, e.g. supporting UK's 77 tech unicorns which may contribute a lot to Gross Value Added bringing benefits mainly to the middle class of the British society (mostly high-skilled workers in the South East).

Bringing British factories from China to Central Europe would also have a positive impact on UK exports, credited by agencies such as UK Export Finance.

UK vs Germany

Comparing the UK engagement in the 3SI countries with the German one, it shows that the UK exports 15 times less ($18 billion vs $269 billion), and import almost seven times less from the region than the Germans ($36 billion vs $243 billion). Obviously Germany is a bit closer than the UK, and has the European Union with its funds but it surprises such a huge scale of trade between these two powers and Central Europe states. After leaving the EU by the United Kingdom, the British are even more needed in the region because of two visions of

Europe: proposed by Germany and France: a European federation (European superpower), and proposed by 3SI countries vision of the EU as a confederation of independent countries. The 3SI countries - who have experienced tyrannies of empires in the past are naturally eager to choose stay independent, doing everything to save its sovereignty that has been more and more limited by Brussels in recent years. Their vision of the EU seems to be a better option for London who does not need a European superpower run by Germany to compete with.

UK vs Russia

Comparing the UK engagement in the 3SI countries with the Russian one we can see that the British export less goods and services to the 3SI states ($18 billion vs $33 billion), and import more than the Russians ($36 billion vs $19 billion). That is a very odd situation considering the fact of existing many restrictions and sanctions in trade between Central Europe and the Russian Federation. There is a huge demand for many British products in the region such as cars and specialised machinery, and the British market enjoys Central European food, electrical machinery, and telecoms and sound equipment. It is really frustrating that Great Britain is unable to trade more with the region than poor Russia, thirty years after economic transformation in the 3SI countries. The main reason for that is a lack of understanding the region in the British government, and treating Central Europe as a less important place than Africa or the Middle East for trade and business. As a result, country such as Poland is the 17th largest trading partner of the UK, the 24th largest export market for British firms, and the 13th largest import market. It is ridiculous that resources are not fully used, great chances to increase British exports are still not made.

Digital

In 2019, the UK exported £207 billion worth of digitally-delivered services, almost two thirds of British total services exports. Cross-border e-commerce sales of goods and services in the same year were worth £118.2 billion.

The UK digital sector employs in 2019 about 1.5 million people and added around £150bn to the British economy. Companies in the digital economy apply their tech and expertise to solve problems and enhance day to day services, providing benefits for consumers across such sectors as food delivery, health, transport, and energy.

Great Britain has an excellent position to cooperate with the 3SI nations in areas such as going paperless, introducing software and focusing on emerging technologies such as cloud computing, big data analytics, and machine learning. They are embracing a digital transformation which is happening both: in the UK and Central Europe.

Switching from paper documents would increase security and transparency in supply chains and provide Governments and the private sector with higher revenues. Great Britain is a leading nation in this matter but also the 3SI countries made big progress in the last decade, e.g. Estonia has created the world's first paperless government – e-Estonia. Today almost 100% of all Estonian state services can be accessed online, and almost all Estonian citizens have an electronic ID card. Nearly 50% of them use internet voting.

The UK is among leaders in terms of paperless education, which is a great goal for schools and universities in Central Europe.

In the contemporary world the speed of internet is a crucial factor to increase firms competitiveness, to go paperless, and to build modern education system. According to cable.co.uk 's

Worldwide broadband speed league 2021, the UK is ranked on 43 position, Hungary is 10th, Poland 31st. We can imagined a 3SI project which could produce analyses why Hungary has faster, and more reliable broadband than Britain, and if we could learn from each other how to build better broadband.

All Europe is building 5G networks facing similar challenges: among three firms which can build it, Nokia, Ericsson, and Huawei, the Chinese corporation was excluded by many European government because of possible national security issues. The 3SI can be used as a platform to work on 5G project to find better cheaper solutions in a cooperation with Ericsson and Nokia.

The largest sub-sector of the digital sector in the UK in terms of contribution to the economy – computer programming, consultancy, and related activities – was home to more than 167.000 firms in 2019.

Transport

There is an urgent need for the UK and the 3SI countries governments for considering more complex trade routes. All forms of transport have a big, unused potential to increase significantly the number of good and passengers between GB and 3SI states.

Freight forwarders look for new land corridors to transport cargo between Asia and Europe. One of them is Polish PKP Cargo Connect that see the greatest opportunities in the main line of the New Silk Road (NJS), which runs through China, Kazakhstan, Russia and Belarus to Poland, and further to Germany, France, and the UK. The firm launched a new intermodal operator connection from Gliwice in Poland to Great Britain via Duisburg in Germany. PKP Cargo Connect also analyses the conditions for launching a rail-ferry connection from Poland to Great Britain in order to significantly facilitate the exchange of goods with the UK. Although Brexit caused a number of problems, it also opened up prospects for logistics operators. Companies like PKP Cargo Connect more and more often cooperate with maritime shipowners because this form of transport become popular (profitable). Although it is longer than the land and ferry, the ports do not have such congestion as at border crossings on the English Channel. For example, Dover is a crucial export/import gateway which handles 17% of the UK's entire trade in goods worth an estimated £122 billion in 2021. It would be a good idea to invest in a 3SI project that helps to connect Polish, Croatian, or Bulgarian ports with other British export/import gateways, increasing trade, and reducing damages from possible blocking Dover as it was in the past (in 2020 France blocked off Dover port).

The United Kingdom is the world's 10th biggest tourist destination, with over 37 million visiting in 2018, including 3.2 million from Poland. Meantime around a million of the British visited Poland the same year, several times less than tourism organisations expect. The main reason for that is not enough transport connections. The 3SI could be a great chance to increase the flow of tourists between the UK and Central Europe.

Energy
There is a lot of space for British engagement in renewable energy projects in the 3SI states, including energy generated from solar, wind, geothermal, hydropower and ocean resources, solid biomass, biogas and liquid biofuels.

In the UK imports of energy were almost twice as large as its exports. Net imports made up 36% of UK energy needs, and the value of gross imports of energy of £45 billion or £18 billion more than gross exports. Gas and oil make up around

90% of energy imports. The 3SI countries have similar issues with imports of energy, and also need to focus more on renewable energy produced domestically.

Electricity generated from wind in the 3SI states in 2020 was equalled to 36.7 billion GWh (UK - 75.6GWh) and has increased their total wind power capacity significantly from 2008. The European Green Deal aims for a 55% reduction of greenhouse gas emissions by 2030 (compared to 1990 levels) and full climate neutrality by 2050. For the energy sector and the 3SI economies, it provides a chance to modernise, innovate and progress, including increased opportunities for investment.

According to Bloomberg Poland is now the best market for green power as it plans to increase its renewable power capacity through the development of offshore wind farms. It's expected that by 2027, 6GW power capacity will be generated by offshore wind in Poland, which is its 2040 energy policy. British energy companies could take part in developing the 3SI markets. Similar challenges are in the UK despite Brexit, and the cooperation can big extremely profitable for firms.

Photovoltaics

Photovoltaics became very popular in the UK as well as in the 3SI countries in the last decade. There has been a sharp decrease in the cost of photovoltaics and European governments introduced many incentive programs toward various groups of society (such as farmers), offering low-interest loans or direct subsidies for the construction of solar power systems. The solar panels production and distribution could become part of the British involvement in the region.

Energy storage

Energy storage industry is also very attractive place for the British investments in the 3SI states. Legal and regulatory barriers that prevented the development of energy storage business have been removed in majority European countries in recent year, creating space for competition. The new rules encourage energy storage by reducing the fee payable by owners and operators of energy storage assets for connecting to the grid. More countries will introduce auctions for hybrid renewable installations, such as facilities combining at least two renewable energy systems and an energy storage facility with a utilisation factor of at least 60%.

Energy storage is a high priority for the UK Government and a key component of the government's push towards a net zero carbon economy. Currently over 16 GW of battery storage capacity is operating, under construction or in the pipeline across 729 projects in the UK.

Conclusion and perspectives

Great Polish writer Witold Gombrowicz wrote in 1954:

"One of the great problems of our culture is opposing Europe. We will not be a truly European nation until we separate ourselves from Europe - because Europeanness does not consist in merging with Europe, but in being its constituent part - specific and irreplaceable ". This thought could be also used if we try to described the British, especially in the context of the Brexit, and if we try to any similarities with the Poles. If there are any.

What we can say for sure is the fact that now is the best time in history to increase contacts between the UK and 3SI nations in all aspects of live: economy, culture, sports etc. The best way to do it is the UK strategic engagement in the 3SI which can bring vast benefits from fast economic growth, increase national security, developing new technologies, and involvement of citizens. If Germany can take advantage from closer cooperation with Central Europe nations, why Britain should not? Brexit can be turned into a great advantage by the UK partnership with the 3SI nations. We want a great strategy of British government regarding the 3SI engagement.

	Total Export	Total Import 2020	UK to 3SI and 3SI to UK	
UK	$837 billion	$877 billion	$18 billion	2.15%
3SI	$977 billion	$966 billion	$36 billion	3.68%

	Area (km2)	Population in ml	Nominal GDP (ml, $) 2020	Nominal GDP per capita ($)
UK	242.500	67.081	3.108	46.200
3SI	1.219.000	111.163	2.073	18.650

Main pros and cons for the 3SI states from their cooperation with The UK:

ADVANTAGES	DISADVANTAGES
Fast economic growth	Mitteleuorpa – an increasing addition from German economy
Increased national security	Brain drain – many talented, young people move to the UK
Development of new technologies	Brexit – the UK outside EU is in a different position as a 3SI states ally.
Nearly 2 millions of the 3SI citizens in the UK.	

Chapter 3 - 3SI & Germany

Why Germany SHOULD NOT be engaged in the 3SI.

Many economists emphasise the fact that the Three Seas Initiative (3SI) is an excellent opportunity for Europe to bridge the economic gap between the Central European countries and Western Europe, between Germany and Poland.

Simultaneously, many experts in geostrategy and geopolitics claim that the 3SI seems to be in contrary with:

- The Russian vision of "spheres of influence", and

- The modified German "Mitteleuropa plan (MEP)" from 1915. The Germans were very sceptical about it from its very beginning. The 3SI that was established a hundred years after the first concepts of the German Mitteleuropa, was described in Berlin as a project that might divide the European Union.

New geopolitical conditions after the demolition of the Berlin Wall, incl

limiting Moscow's influence changed Germany's position in relation to its

eastern neighbours. The economic power of the united Germany and its traditional interest in the situation beyond its eastern border contribute to the strengthening of contacts between Poland, Hungary or the Czech Republic and Germany.[9]

Germany is one of the main world powerhouses and its economy is a colossus in comparison with any Central European economies. But what happens if we compare German Gross Domestic Product ($4.3 trillion) with the combined GDP of all the 3SI states ($2.1 trillion), and impressive value of German exports ($2 trillion) with the 3SI

---

[9] Piotr Eberhardt: „The genesis of the German concept of 'Mitteleuropa', p. 21

states exports ($0.98 trillion)? The 3SI production and trade are half of the German ones. Also pretty good!

The first half of 1990s was very hard for peoples of the Central Europe: a fast transformation of their economies from communism to capitalism caused huge crises with unbelievably high rate of unemployment, hyperinflation, and huge imbalance in foreign trade. After this shock, Central Europe started developing rapidly, and the economic boom was held in that part of the world after accessing the European Union by those countries in 2004.

Meantime, Western Germany were united with Eastern Germany in 1990, which was a great political success but the whole process last years, and cost a fortune, significantly slowing down German economy. After joining the euro area, the economic situation of Germany was assessed very critically, both at home and abroad. Between 1991 and 2001 unemployment in Germany, especially in the new federal states, remained at a high level of 20%, the public debt grew, and the payment deficit in economic exchange with foreign countries persisted. Germany together with France were the first to break the budget deficit rules in force in the Euro area. The united Germany was straggling for many years till 2004, when new members joined the European Union. Those Central European countries immediately became important trade partners for Germany, and a favourite place for German firms to build their factories. Cooperation between Germany and Central Europe has been increasing every year since that, bringing benefits to all participants. However, not everything looks so great. Current socioeconomic ties between Berlin and Central Europe capitals may remind us about the main objectives of the old German Mitteleuropa plan from 1915.

Mitteleuropa plan

The concept of Mitteleuropa plan (MEP) was created by German Joseph Partsch, who wrote a book called: Mitteleuropa before the First World War. He defined the geographical boundaries of the MEP between the North Sea, the Baltic Sea, the Black Sea and the Adriatic. It covered two Empires: German and Austro-Hungarian, and most of the Balkan Peninsula with Serbia, Romania and Bulgaria. Partsch also added Switzerland, Belgium and the Netherlands as part of the MEP arguing that the Germans dominate in these territories and are natural leaders who can laid a solid foundation for building a great state. He and other influential Germans who shaped the concept of the MEP, seen that superpower under German leadership as a necessary step before the inevitable confrontation with Russia.

In 1915 another German intellectual, Friedrich Naumann also wrote a book titled: "Mitteleuropa" that was published in a moment, when the German army won a series of victories on the Eastern Front. F. Naumann's concept of the MEP was a combination of the German and the Austro-Hungarian Empires, supported by Turkey, Bulgaria and Romania, and included the Baltic nations. He believed in contrary to Partsch, that there was no need for the Germanization of countries in Central and Eastern Europe, which should be independent but bind with strong political and economic ties with Germany. According to Naumann they would naturally gravitate to the centre of power in Berlin. Nauman's MEP was based on the assumption that building a new political architecture in Central Europe is necessary for Germany to gain a dominant position in Europe, and then to become a world power.

As we know Germany started and lost both World Wars, and then the Soviet Union dominated Central and Eastern Europe between 1945 and 1991, therefore Nauman's Mitteleuropa had to be left for later.

After the unification of both German states in 1990, and the Soviet Union collapse in 1991, German strategists modified the Mitteleuropa plan (MEP) adjusting it to the German great plan - the European Union.

It's hard to find the MEP directly in the contemporary German politics. However if we look closer into economic relations between Germany and individual Central European countries we can easily see that those states have been permanently cemented with German economy in recent years. Germany became the most important trade partner (exports and imports), and the biggest investor (Foreign Direct Investments) for all 3SI countries. For example: Czech Republic sells 1/3 of its exports to Germany, and imports a quarter. German combined exports to France and Italy is smaller than exports to the 3SI countries. A large part of German supply chains are located in the 3SI, including the production of final goods, and the region is a crucial resource of labour force.

However, it should be remembered that Germany's domination in Central and Eastern Europe is a double-edged sword. Germany would not be such a powerful country without the facilities it enjoys from cheaper labour in relatively nearby countries. The economic prosperity of Central and Eastern Europe has fuelled and will continue to drive the German economy. The inhabitants of the region should realize how strong their ties with Germany are, but the German elite should also make their own examination of conscience, because the countries of Central and Eastern Europe are no longer the same organisms as twenty-five years ago. Their ambitions are growing.[10]

---

[10] teologiapolityczna.pl/lukasz-jasina-europa-srodkowa-niemcy-czyli-jak-gospodarka-wplywa-na-polityke

German firms helped in the modernisation of whole region, gaining significant market shares in such sectors as digital, transport, and energy. Their investments in the region became an important source of improving the international competitiveness of the German economy, and an element of cost reduction of the production, as well as the pressure exerted by business on German workers to reduce labour costs. Germany's enterprises attracted thousands of skilled workers from the region to Germany, and carried part of the research activities to Central Europe, dealing that way with a big problem of the shortage a sufficient number of engineers. Investments financed from the European funds also have positive contribution to the economic cooperation between Germany and Central Europe. Germany were the largest beneficiary of investments in the region, getting financial support from the EU funds allocated to the European Union cohesion policy, which added billions of euros to German export to those countries. German firms supported with the EU money won many contracts on the development of infrastructure, building motorways that connected Germany and Central and Eastern Europe.

The 3SI countries maintained relatively balanced trade relations, showing a surplus in trade with Germany, which proves their efficiency to produce high quality components and goods for German companies especially in the automotive, electromechanical and retail sectors. This is more and more often followed by the transfer of German R&D to the 3SI states, which results in higher products added value. In addition to the traditional advantages of Central Europe, such as geographical proximity, industrial production traditions, low labour costs, and reliability of deliveries, it's equality important the region's economic stability, political development, good infrastructure, as well as mentioned before, highly qualified and efficient labour force.

Current economic instability in the world (Covid-19, tensions between USA and China) increases the importance of Central Europe for Germany. Region's geographic proximity ensures economic cooperation, and avoids geopolitical problems. There is also no risk of interrupting the continuity of supplies, which is unfortunately a case in terms of supplies from the Far East.

Another very important advantage of the region is a fact that all the 3SI nations are in the EU, so German firms can treat them as a single market with many similarities such as:
   a) uniform market rules valid throughout the EU, significant share of foreign capital in the manufacturing and financial sectors;
   b) an economic model based on exports with a significant share of foreign companies;
   c) low or insignificant resources of raw materials and high dependence on their import;
   d) significant resources of qualified employees with lower salary expectations than in Germany;
   e) good economic results compared to the rest of the EU during the global financial crisis in 2008.

Thanks to low wages, well-educated labour force, and high productivity Central Europe produces goods for German firms not only directed for the EU markets - the production of which would be too expensive if transferred to China due to costs of transport, but also a significant part of the 3SI states exports to Germany is re-exported to China.

In response to the diagnosis of German economists who blamed the excessively high labour costs as a main issue in terms of reducing economic competitiveness, the German government introduced the Agenda 2010 package of reforms, limiting social benefits, improving the conditions for running a business and making the market more flexible work. German trade unions under pressure of reforms and threats to transfer jobs from Germany to the 3SI countries limited their wage expectations, focusing on maintaining plants in Germany.

The German sector of small and medium-sized enterprises is largely involved in the cooperation with the 3SI economies, because these countries have similar legal and tax regulations to German, with high standards of legal protection. They specially invested their capital in production of spare parts to cars and machines. German automotive corporations expanded their production to the 3SI countries further after 2009, being pleased with high efficiency of car factories that already existed there. German firms investments in the 3SI countries resulted in vast penetration of local markets and establishing dominant positions there.

In the recent years German companies more often see Central Europe as a good place to locate investments in the research and development (R&D), recognising the region as equally competitive and attractive as locations in France and Italy. The 3SI countries are often chosen to build R&D centres, as German firms prefer to have them close geographically to their factories, and countries like China or India seem to be too distant.

An important issue in the 3SI countries is aging and decreasing population, as a result of migration (brain drain) to Germany in last decades. In 2019 Germany (with total population of over 83 million, including foreign nationals of 11.5 million) was a home for 867.000 Poles, 799.000 Romanians, 427.000 Croatians, 389.000 Bulgarians, 211.000 Hungarians, any many others. Many of them are young engineers, doctors, and business people, who could contribute to their birth place country economies if they stayed in Prague, Budapest or Sofia.

Transport

After the enlargement of the EU, Germany strengthen its position in the 3SI countries' transport of goods between east and west of the continent, and German firms aimed to be key intermediaries in trade with the region. Logistics companies first largely profit from the transportation of components and raw materials from Central Europe, then earn from transporting finished products that flowed in reverse direction (from Germany to the 3SI economies). They established their subsidiaries in the region following clients from the German automotive and electromechanical industries, offering them their services.

Digital

Germany is one of the fastest-growing markets for technology and the IT industry covering around 25% of the European market, leading in such technologies as blockchain, Internet of Things, and big data. German software industry had 27.5 billion euros revenue in 2020. Germany has been one of the fastest-growing markets for technology and the IT industry. When it comes to adapting groundbreaking new technology like blockchain, IoT as well as big data, Germany covers more than one-fourth of the European market.

The revenue of the software industry in Germany was estimated to be about 27.5 billion euros in 2020. Berlin is the second biggest start-up hub in Europe, with numerous globally recognised technology companies (Reis Robotics, NanoAndMore, BenQ Mobile), which headquarters are located in less than 200 km from the borders of the 3SI. Thousands of engineers, programmers, and designers from the twelve 3SI states work for them in Germany and in central Europe. The close relationship between Germany and the 3SI nations in the IT sector has arisen from a mix of various factors: highly qualified professionals, good language skills, open, global economy, and outsourcing.

Energy

German energy companies are also important players in the 3SI markets. However, German energy transformation after 2011 (the Fukushima power plant failure case), caused a great confusion for the whole European energy industry. The compulsory closure of the German nuclear power plants and their gradual withdrawal from the market by 2023 overlaps with the covid-19 crisis in Europe, that first significantly decreased the demand for electricity, reducing the profits of energy companies, and then increased prices significantly in 2021/22. Main German companies such as E.ON and RWE had to change their sources of revenues that were generated from traditional sources (nuclear, gas, coal), focusing on the renewable energy sources, which is a long term and capital intensive process. After 2019 German energy firms started selling off some of their assets in Central Europe decreasing investments in the region, and trying to generate savings transferring some of their jobs from Germany to the 3SI countries, e.g. establishing shared service centres. Generally they have been weakening their position in the 3SI in recent years but still staying important players in the region, controlling several largest energy suppliers, power plants, and gas networks. For example, in Poland RWE is one of the largest foreign investors being the fifth largest energy supplier, investing in the gas sector, wind farms, and the transmission networks. In Slovakia, RWE is the third largest energy supplier, and the second largest gas. In Hungary RWE is the second largest energy supplier.

The Nord Stream

German energy firms engagement in the Nord Stream gas pipe line that supplies gas from Russia to Germany on the bottom of the Baltic Sea, poisons economic and political prelateship with Central Europe states. The project is controlled in 51% by Russian Gazprom, 20% by German firms Wintershall (controlled by BASF), and E.ON – also 20%. These firms want to re-sell Russian gas to the 3SI in a situation when the region (and the rest of Europe) urgently need to reduce their dependency from Russian oil and gas.

The fact that Germany has a block of the 3SI countries on its eastern border, that are also members of the NATO and the European Union, increase its National Security, and allows the central government in Berlin spend much less on military forces. The only potential threat for Germany is the Russian Federation, which is a bigger danger for countries such as Poland and Romania. Because of that Germany spent on its military forces only 1.4% of GDP (£53 billion) in 2020, compare to Romania 2.3% (£5.7 billion), Poland 2.2% (£13 billion), and Latvia 2.3% (£0.8 billion). If Central Europe would not be part of the NATO and the EU, Germany would have to spend at least additional $26 billion per year on its army. Military could be possibly a good area to extend cooperation between the 3SI states and Germany, as Berlin is an important exporter of weapon, with a revenue of $1.2 billion in 2020.

Conclusion & Recommendations

The 3SI leaders should be aware of the possible risks, which cooperation with Germany brings. At the moment, a profitable cooperation in the European Union structures satisfy all sides, but the future may bring less fortunate circumstances.

German establishment never mentions about Neuman's Mitteleuropa plan publicly, but some of the political leaders in Berlin openly admire Otto von Bismarck – chancellor of the German empire between 1871-1890 – who believed that Germany should closely cooperate with Russia, sharing spheres of influence in Europe. Moreover, current rules of Kremlin like that idea too seeing in Germany valuable partner. The 3SI states need to reduce their dependency on Germany by remodelling their economies, building new engines of economic growth.

The Three Seas Initiative had a fairly good understanding of the scale of cementing economic relations with Germany and their importance for individual economies. The 3SI economies are not diversified, and established strict relationships with Germany as Nauman predicted in his book.

	Total Export	Total Import 2020	Germany to 3SI, 3SI to Germany	
Germany	$2.004 billion	$1.8 trillion	$269 billion	13.42%
3SI	$977 billion	$966 billion	$243 billion	24.87%

	Area (km2)	Population in ml	Nominal GDP ($) 2020	Nominal GDP per capita
Germany	357.000	83.240	4.319 tln	57.000
3SI	1.219.000	111.163	2.073 tln	18.650

Main pros and cons for the 3SI states from their cooperation with Germany:

ADVANTAGES	DISADVANTAGES
Fast economic growth	Mitteleuropa – an increasing

	addition from German economy
Increased national security	Brain drain – most talented, young people move to Germany
Development of new technologies	Nord Stream pact – a dangerous cooperation Germany - Russia

Chapter 4 - 3SI & China

Why China SHOULD NOT be engaged in the 3SI

Central and Eastern Europe region is probably the last in the world without significant Chinese investments, and is remaining quite unknown in China. When the Central European countries emerged unscathed from the economic crisis in 2008, it was noticed in Beijing and China began looking for a new format of cooperation with the region. The result of that was introducing the 16+1 formula in 2012 in Warsaw, after months of consultations.

Although, China is not sure how to deal with Central Europe it decided to gain a foothold in the region, and gain new markets for its businesses, as well as to improve its image in the EU.

According to an analysis by the CSIS Reconnecting Asia Project, China has contributed around $15.4 billion toward infrastructure and other investment in the 16+1 countries between 2012 and 2018.

China is eight times bigger than all 12 3SI countries, is thirteen times more populated, its economy is eight time bigger but its GDP per capita is $7.000 smaller than average in the 3SI states.

The first contacts between the Central Europe and China can be dated at the XIII century when Benedict of Poland, a Franciscan friar, and explorer accompanied Giovanni da Pian del Carpine in his journey as delegate of Pope Innocent IV to the Great Khan Güyük of the Mongol Empire in 1245-1247. To compare: famous Marco Polo travelled through Asia along the Silk Road between 1271 and 1295, and in 1205 the Mongols conquered Beijing establishing the Yuan dynasty. One of the things which surprised him was a fact that he met in the City of Karakorum many Europeans, for example the Grand Prince of Kiev Yaroslav II.

Another important person who contributed to re-establishing historical relations between China and Central Europe was Michał Boym who was sent by a Polish king to the court of Emperor Yongli in 1649.

He came to the imperial court at the time of the Ming Dynasty crisis and its fall to the Manchus of the new Qing Dynasty. Boym became an imperial envoy who traveled back to Europe to enlist aid for the Yongli. By the time Boym went back to China, the fall of the last Ming emperor was doomed. It is true that he reached China, but failed to provide the emperor with an answer. This one, however, contained no particulars, only vague promises from the Portuguese.[11]

Many times happened that China assumed that Central Europe, including the Balkans and the Baltic states could be treated somewhat similarly to the Third World countries, today called developing countries. Central Europe and China don't know and don't understand each other.

The Chinese president Xi used to refer the cooperation with the CEE region as cooperation with the Global South, until advisers explained him that it was not taken as a compliment in the region. It took some time for this understanding to descend to a lower level of the Chinese administration.

This mutual ignorance of intentions was perhaps due to the fact that both sides simply knew little about each other. The ignorance of the completely different business philosophy driving the two sides was considerable.

---

[11]https://historia.org.pl/2019/09/26/historia-nawiazania-stosunkow-dyplomatycznych-pomiedzy-polska-a-chinska-republika-ludowa/

Mr. Jakub Jakóbowski from the Center for Eastern Studies recalls that a Chinese business delegation came to Warsaw a few years ago to meet Polish businessmen, attracted by the opportunity to do business with China. The Chinese presented their offers: chemicals, heavy industry, plastic and other "dirty" sectors. Confused participants of the meeting replied that Poland was in the European Union and not only would it not be profitable for them to import such things, but even we could not, because we were bound by the legal EU regulations. This response clearly surprised the Chinese, who replied that they had just returned from Iraq and Mozambique, and there was enthusiasm for similar ideas.

For these and other reasons, the idea of a smooth cooperation between the region and China remain a big challenge: the combination of countries so different, on many levels: the Balkans, the Baltic states, Central Europe, through cultural issues (various religious bases, from Catholicism to Orthodoxy, and different pace of secularization of societies), legal (EU members and the rest) to political (attitudes from clearly anti-Russian to pro-Russian). Such a grouping of countries immediately showed China's poor knowledge of this part of the world. The lack of Chinese experience, lack of a regional policy, and the lack of details is clearly visible. In addition, there was a lack of enthusiasm towards China, noticeable in several EU countries, because nothing it does not break the EU's unity towards China as much as the particular interests negotiated in Beijing by its biggest players. Another problem that stood in the way of closer cooperation with Central Europe are poor development of existing rail connections between China and Europe, customs procedures, differences in rail systems, shortage of goods that can be exported to China and the fact that it is still cheaper to ship goods by sea, the limitation of the policy of some countries towards China as a result of EU membership, from smaller issues (trade barriers or visa policies) to larger issues, such as matching the economies of the region as subcontractors of the German economy, small and medium-sized enterprises from Central Europe are not good partners for the great Chinese state-owned corporations. Moreover, the economic structure and market dominance by Western companies in the region also limits possible cooperation, as 90% of Central Europe exports to China are produced by multinational corporations.

US and China rivalry
US and China rivalry matters most as good relations with the US being a priority for Central European states. The increasing rivalry between two powers put the region in a difficult situation because the USA is the main national security guarantor for these countries.
The Americans take advantage of the pro-American attitude of Central Europe, and began to block Chinese influence in this region of the world. Thus, the deterioration in Washington-Beijing relations had a direct impact on the weakening of enthusiasm towards China in a large part of the 1 + 16 initiative.
Central Europe has two attractive opportunities for their further development: the Chinese Silk Road also called Belt and Road, and the European Union.
The mere entry of China does not improve the region's position automatically. Contrary to the dreams of some economists, the appearance of Chinese capital will not prevent the 1 + 16 countries from avoiding the middle-development trap (to avoid which, they need to switch to highly advanced products and services). The Chinese presence in the region is still not big, and in terms of investments, the

Chinese are behind not only Western countries, but also Asian competitors such as Japan, South Korea and Taiwan (the Chinese presence is more noticeable on the Balkans). The large political hype by no means translated into a stronger economic presence.

New Silk Road

There is no coincidence that just a year after introducing the 1+16 initiative China announced in 2013 its New Silk Road project (Belt and Road), which can have a major impact on Central Europe, similar to the integration with the European Union. In the second decade of the XXI century China feels strong enough to challenge the United States of America in the global supremacy, and to do so, it needs the New Silk Road as the master plan, and the 1+16 (later 1+17) Initiative as one of its subprojects (among its many bilateral and multilateral initiatives).

New Silk Road (NSR) is considered to be a continuance of the ancient trade route that once ran indirectly between China and Europe, and its purpose is to reopen a trade corridor with many channels between China, Central Asia, the Middle East and Europe.

According to the Belt and Road Action Plan, it will encompass land routes (the "Belt") and maritime routes (the "Road") with the goal of improving trade relationships with other states, primarily through infrastructure investments. According to the Chinese government the NSR is worth $900 billion, and is to kindle a golden age of commerce that will benefit all. China is planning to lend $8 trillion for infrastructure in 68 countries, adding up to as much as 65% of the global population and a third of global GDP.

So far, the opinions from the rest of the world about the NSR have been mixed, with several countries expressing their disappointment of differences between ambitious plans and reality.

New Silk Road has its weaknesses, the foggy nature, and goals that are unclearly defined. The Chinese like to talk about this as a long term project for decades, which according to Dr Lubina from the Univeristy of Warsaw, fits well with the popular myth of the Chinese as people planning many years ahead (the Chinese leaders did not foresee the outbreak of the housing crisis events in Hong Kong or even that pro-Beijing parties would fall in local elections). However, such slogans are ideally suited for propaganda purposes.

Despite of the fact that the NSR has proved to be expensive and controversial, countries in Central and Eastern Europe hope that it will have a positive, economic impact on their economies.

The 16+1 Initiative

The 16+1 Initiative summits happen annually: in February 2021 virtually because of the pandemic, and before in Dubrovnik (2019), Sofia (2018), Budapest (2017), Riga (2016), Suzhou (2015), Belgrade (2014), Bucharest (2013) and Warsaw (2012). The China-Central Europe secretariat is in Beijing, with 16 "national coordinators" in each of the partner Central Europe countries.

The 16 countries are: Albania, Bosnia and Herzegovina, Bulgaria, Croatia, the Czech Republic, Estonia, Greece, Hungary, Latvia, North Macedonia, Montenegro, Poland, Romania, Serbia, Slovakia and Slovenia. Greece joined the 16+1 Initiative in 2019, and Lithuania left it in 2021. In comparison to the Three Seas Initiative, ten countries are members in both organisations: Bulgaria, Croatia, the Czech

Republic, Estonia, Hungary, Latvia, Poland, Romania, Slovakia and Slovenia.

The format goals to promote enhance cooperation in infrastructure, transportation and logistics, trade and investment. It is supposed to help grow ties in the areas such as culture, education, tourism, cultural exchanges, think tanks and NGOs.

The 1 + 16 has started reviving contacts between China and the region, and the Chinese created a new bank for Central and Eastern Europe in 2015, that helps to develop infrastructure, logistics, industry and agriculture. The Chinese goal is to stimulate infrastructure exports (China has created the world's largest infrastructure industry and wants to keep employment in it by exporting the sale of infrastructure services), for which the region is perfectly suited. The economic orientation of cooperation with the region was expressed by the fact that Li Keqiang (responsible for the domestic economy in China) came to most of the 16+1 summits, not Xi Jinping, who deals with internal politics. Another reason for China's interest was the perception of the region as a potential transit point for Chinese goods (however, the lack of communication lines, especially the North-South, as well as different gauges of railway lines or the lack of electrification, were a major obstacle to this goal from the very beginning). Apart from geography, from Beijing's point of view, the lack of historical problems in relations with these countries was important, and the Chinese believed that the people of Central Europe would be won by the hopes of grants, loans and investments.

In response to such actions by China, some of the countries belonging to the group began to see it as their chance. In 2015-2016, there was widespread hope that Polish companies would enter the Chinese market. The informal Polish strategy indicated an attempt to enter the poorer Chinese provinces, not yet dominated by Western capital, such as Sichuan, Ningxia, Gansu or Qinghai; this was a fairly correct assumption, as the interior and west of China are areas where it would be easier to break through than on the east or south coast of China, where Western companies have been investing for over 20 years. In any case, people believed in opportunities in sectors and industries as well as in the development of trade. The flagship example for that was the Changdu - Łódź connection, thanks to which goods can be delivered in less than 2 weeks. This train connection was discussed almost constantly in the second decade of the 21st century. At every meeting, from political, through local government, to academic and social, the topic of the train appeared invariably, and always positively. The train connection was considered as the main achievement and main hope in Polish-Chinese contacts, it was constantly argued about its advantages: 4 times shorter than sea transport and much cheaper than air transport.

The reloading train hub in Małaszewicze near the Belarusian border was discussed with similar enthusiasm, and equally frequently. These two specific examples were linked to the broader "geopolitical" vision, promoted since at least 2015, according to which China's entry into the region was to become a structural change for its countries. In this perspective, the inflow of Chinese capital was to be the third most important for the region, after Western capital in 1989 and the EU capital after 2004, which used the favourable geography of Central Europe, and created new connections on the North-South line. As a result, there would be an accumulation of capital, which would give the region a subjectivity. Unfortunately, these expectations did not happen so far.

According to the report of the German think tank Mercator Institute for 2019 China Studies, the total value of Chinese investments in 12 CEE EU countries belonging to the 16+1 initiative in the years 2000–2019 amounted to less than €9.5 billion (of which €1.4 billion in Poland). For comparison, in this period, the Chinese side invested in Germany itself almost €23 billion, almost €6 billion in Italy, and also €6 billion of Chinese investments in Portugal.

The most important decisions regarding economic cooperation between China and the region are undertaken on a bilateral level, which strengthens the impression that the 16+1 does not fulfil its declared function.

16+1 has a weak basis for development, because there is a lack of a good offer from China that could increase exports from Central Europe. From the economic point of view, the initiative is completely unattractive to the participants as the Chinese trials to adapt policies to individual partners are mostly ineffective. Central Europe is simply focused on maintaining tense relationships with the US and the EU whose policies are usually competitive to the Chinese ones.

It manifests itself mainly in relation to the threats related to the participation of Chinese companies in the construction of the 5G networks. In the context of infrastructure, Romania, for example, blocked the Chinese investment in the nuclear power plant in Cernavoda, and also plans to prohibit Chinese companies from participating in infrastructure tenders due to the lack of similar access to the Chinese market for EU companies. The Greek government did not agree to the participation of Chinese companies in the tender for the purchase of one of the power grid operators. Poland, Romania and Slovakia are working on regulations that will in practice prohibit Chinese companies from participating in the construction of the 5G networks.

Despite dissatisfaction with the results, EU members treat the 16+1 as a channel of political communication with China, as well as a chance for domestic businesses to enter that country with their products.

Only a few countries such as Hungary, Serbia and North Macedonia emphasize the positive effects of cooperation with China in the 16+1 so far. All three countries purchased Chinese vaccines against COVID-19, and the Hungarian government decided to establish a branch of the Fudan university in Budapest by 2024. These countries decided to cooperate with China not only because of its economic importance, but also as an element of diversifying the directions of foreign policy.

China has proposed to call 2021 the year of "Green China-Central Europe cooperation", which, however, contrasts with Chinese investments in coal-fired power plants, including those in the Balkans. China tries to develop bilateral relations in less controversial areas: culture, science, tourism, and sport (especially in the context of promoting the Beijing Winter Olympics in 2022).

Completing the negotiations of the Investment Agreement with the EU (CAI) in December 2020 was a great political success for China, and the swift ratification of the agreement is their priority. Due to negative sentiment towards the CAI in the European Parliament, which has to accept the agreement, China does not want to worsen relations with the EU, and will not strengthen the 16+1 initiative through development of regional cooperation projects with European countries in order to strengthen relations with the entire EU.

During the virtual 16+1 summit in February 2021 Central Europe countries were represented at the lowest level since their inception (as many as six of them limited themselves to the participation of ministers). Moreover, for the first time the final document has not been adopted due to the reluctance of some countries. Instead, only the '2021 Action Plan' was approved, containing mainly a list of events. President Xi in his speech emphasized the will of further cooperation and also declared that the value of imports from the region would double within 5 years.

The development of trade between China and the countries of the region has almost doubled in the last decade, while the Chinese imports from the region is 25% higher than exports. China-Europe Railway Express has handled over 30,000 freight transports to the region so far. China intends to import over $170 billion worth of goods from the 16+1 partners over the next five years and to double imports of agricultural products from Central Europe. The Chinese media presented the summit and cooperation between China and the CEE countries as a success. According to the Ministry of Commerce of China, in 2020 the total trade volume between China and Central Europe reached over $103 billion, recording an 8.4% increase and exceeding the threshold of $100 billion for the first time.

Chinese plans to import $170 billion worth of goods from the region may be difficult to achieve, especially given its "double circulation" strategy aimed at the internal market. Many successful Chinese projects such as e.g. the expansion of the Greek Port of Piraeus or the modernization of the Budapest-Belgrade railway line, are just the result of bilateral agreements and bilateral arrangements.

The 16 countries are treated by China as an addition to European policy but want they really want from Beijing are infrastructure (greenfield) investments, to create jobs and industrial production, hence the takeovers and interest in the logistics and construction industries. From this point of view, Chinese loans and grants turned out to be unattractive.

China's entry into the region has not brought a radical change, and there is only a little improvement in political relations owning to a 15-minute meeting with the Chinese prime minister during the summits, which provided a certain level of communication, but mainly simply courtesy. As a result, disappointment was growing in the region, especially among countries such as Poland and the Czech Republic, which engaged considerable political capital in relations with China and little resulted from it.

The 16 countries did not get what they wanted: neither the technology, nor the opening up of the Chinese market, getting a poorly tailored Chinese offer, that is beneficial only for China, and adapted to the countries of the Global South, while countries such Poland, Hungary or the Baltic states, after 30 years of transformation have found themselves in the Global North and not only do not identify themselves with the Global South, but their economies are already at a different level of interdependence.

A positive thing about the 16+1 is the fact that China and these countries have finally met. Not only politicians and businessmen, but also journalists, actors, musicians.

Hopefully, the Chinese learned from their failure. Or maybe not. The Chinese Prime Minister Li Keqiang invited the Germans to participate in the 16+1 without any consultations with the 16.

Another challenge is the asymmetry of economic needs and expectations on both sides. China is aware of the existence of a huge trade deficit that will not be offset by bilateral actions. The golden period of investing in the region, in which foreign investors had access to attractive, privatized assets, is over. Currently, the countries of the region are counting on greenfield investments, which are too risky for some Chinese companies.[12]

Transport

Transport and transportation in the 3SI is very important sector of economy, and will play a crucial role in the future, connecting Asia and Europe. One of the possible threats for the 3SI countries is a situation when Chinese goods destine to Western Europe would pass the region without any benefits for the 3SI states. Although Central Europe has a favourable geographical position, without reloading goods in this area, the trains with Chinese goods will simply pass the region on the way to Germany or France, and no greater benefits will arise.

An interesting example of Chinese-Polish cooperation is the case of the Chinese company Covec, which after many disagreements with Polish subcontractors, abandoned the construction of the A2 motorway. The failure of this company resulted rather from the lack of communication and mutual stereotypes: it can be said that the Poles believed that the Chinese would build a road for a "bowl of rice", while the Chinese thought that they would earn for "ignorant locals like in Africa". This story had bad consequences for years, but it could be a case study for new investors.

Closer relations with Hungary and Serbia will allow China avoid similar misunderstandings, and the Chinese are successfully building the Belgrade-Budapest railway connection.

Digital

Digital (hi-tech) sector is the place in the 3SI countries where the most active Chinese corporation Huawei declared its

---

¹² https://www.osw.waw.pl/pl/publikacje/komentarze-osw/2015-04-14/chiny-europa-srodkowo-wschodnia-161-widziane-z-pekinu

strong commitment to the technological development, especially in Poland. Huawei is particularly interested in projects in education sector (delivery of a super-fast Internet systems), and helping in the digital transformation of cultural activities and traditional business models, such as high-speed connectivity services.

Huawei is accused by Washington to be a threat for national security, and connection with the Chinese secret service. However, the firm is one of the three corporations in the world (together with Nokia and Erickson) that has technologies and competencies to build the 5G networks.

Romania, Poland, Estonia, Latvia, the Czech Republic, Slovenia, Albania, Lithuania, Greece, Bulgaria, Slovakia, North Macedonia and Serbia have signed memoranda of understanding with the United States on this issue or joined the Washington Clean Network initiative. This is one of the more sensitive topics for China, and a clear sign of the scepticism of the 3SI countries regarding deeper cooperation with China which resulted in limiting the possibilities of Huawei to build national 5G networks infrastructure in the region.

In this context, it looks like Central Europe does not want to completely resign from cooperation with the Chinese, but tries to balance its own interests and the most important foreign partners. It is visible in the debate on the role of Huawei in building the 5G networks in Poland: although Warsaw declares close cooperation with Washington in terms of maintaining the safety of the native

telecommunications networks (what from the perspective of the US means restricting Huawei's share), this does not mean exclusion of this Chinese company from the Polish market. The Polish government wants to avoid becoming dependent from one supplier of such crucial technology as 5G and focuses on diversification.

Energy
In terms of energy sector in the 3SI states China did some attempts to be present in the region but energy became a sensitive area of national security in Europe. Romania has withdrawn from the agreement with China on the construction of nuclear reactors at the Cernavoda power plant and the Czech Republic's government decided that Chinese companies should not participate in the tender for the construction of a new nuclear power plant in that country. Poland considers firms from the USA, France and South Korea as business partners to build its first nuclear plant.

Conclusion and perspectives
This 16+1 evolution, from a peculiar bridgehead in the EU to China's game with Germany and its way of influencing the hard core of the European Union showed well how China operates on the international stage: its style of functioning. In the structures it creates, resembling an iceberg, China moves where there is a will to cooperate, and stops where there is a blockage. In other words, it is adjusting to current conditions, not pushing yourself where you can, but going where you can. It can be said that it looks quite clumsy - because they announce some announcements, plans, initiatives, and then not much comes out of it. But on the other hand, the Chinese are flexible because of it, they change their center of gravity depending on the situation. This corresponds perfectly to what is called tifa in Chinese, or "state strategy guidelines": a peculiar meta-principle that defines the goals of Chinese policy, according to the principle of "obedience to the party line, but with the necessary flexibility." Tifa is a universal tool

of Chinese politics. 1+16 (17) confirmed a certain way of China's behaviour in international relations.[13]

In 2021, the importance of the region in China's foreign policy will decrease. This is due not only to changes in the perception of the 16+1 format by its European participants, but also Because Beijing had to focus more on its domestic market, and the reduction in financing Chinese foreign investments including the Belt and Road.

The growing deficit in trade with China is also an important factor when we talk about tightening ties with Central Europe (in 2019 it amounted to a record $20 billion).

Chinese entrepreneurs lack knowledge and practical expertise about the region. Analysts point to insufficient recognition of the legal environment and the specificity of the region, which contributes to the weak competitive position of Chinese companies. It is indicated that it is a matter of little experience in cooperation, insufficient knowledge of the legal environment, labour and investment law and the social environment, e.g. the mentality of the local workforce.

Despite numerous constraints such as the increasing deficit in trade with China, and a rising conflict between the USA and China, the 3SI countries most like will increase their participation in the Chinese Silk Road, absorbing more investment from that superpower.

	Total Export	Total Import 2020	China to 3SI, 3SI to China	
China	$2.590 billion	$2.060 billion	$70 billion	2.70%
3SI	$977 billion	$966 billion	$32 billion	3.28%

	Area (km2)	Population	Nominal GDP (2020)	Nominal GDP per capita

---

[13] https://usa-ue.pl/teksty-i-komentarze/teksty/pokraczne-wejscie-smoka-chiny-i-format-116-17/ - Michał Lubina

| China | 9.597.000 | 1.402.000.000 | $16.6 tln | $11.819 |
| 3SI | 1.219.000 | 111.163.000 | $2.1 tln | $18.650 |

Main pros and cons for the 3SI states from their cooperation with Germany:

ADVANTAGES	DISADVANTAGES
Participation in the New Silk Road	An increasing imbalance in trade
Chinese influence on Russia & Germany	Conflict China - USA
Development of new technologies	
Culture, arts, sports	

Chapter 5 - 3SI & Russia

Why Russia SHOULD NOT be engaged in the 3SI.

Russia has treated Central and Eastern Europe as own sphere of influence since at least the XVIII century when tsar Peter I (its ruler between 1682-1725) and later Catherine II (ruler between 1762-1796) strengthened that country by conducting thorough reforms, lifting it to the position of the regional power, by weakening and destroying its main rival Poland, and then establishing Russian empire. After the Second World War the Soviet Union terrorised and exploited Central European states from Estonia to Bulgaria for nearly fifty years. Since president Putin became a Russian leader in year 2000, he openly expressed many times his will to restore the Russian Empire, claiming that the collapse of the Soviet Union was the biggest tragedy in history. The Three Seas Initiative (3SI) countries being members of the European Union, and the NATO (all except Austria) feel saver after 2004, but it became clear for them that closer cooperation in the region is necessary to increase their national security further.

Russia's population (144 millions) is bigger than the population of all 12 3SI countries (111 millions), but the Soviet Union had 289 millions of inhabitants in 1991. The 3SI combined gross domestic product is higher ($2.1 trillion) than the Russian one ($1.7 trillion), as well as 3SI exports ($977 billion) compare to Russian exports ($551 billion). Trade between the Russian Federation and the 3SI could be increased two or three times in the next two decades, but there is no political will to do so. The Soviet mentality on the Kremlin blocks international trade in that region of the world.

Sphere of influence

"The Near abroad" is a term used by the Russians to refer to the countries that used to be part of the Russian Empire and the Soviet Union, which Russia considers as their sphere of influence, which means former soviet republics, as well as countries formerly belonging to the Council for Mutual Economic Aid and the Warsaw Pact (the Eastern bloc).

According to the Swedish Security Service (SAPO) Russia has developed the doctrine of the shadow economy, which means that it wants to influence Sweden, Finland, and Central European countries without causing an armed conflict. As part of it, sensitive data is constantly collected and can be used to destabilize these countries if necessary. Russia is trying to achieve its goals through information propaganda campaigns, cyber-attacks, as well as acquisitions of strategic companies and technologies.

The Russian Federation builds its sphere of influence mainly on the basis of the export of its natural resources such as oil and gas. Due to the supply of such strategic goods, it can exert effective political influence on its neighbouring countries. For example, in recent years countries such as Belarus, Ukraine and Moldova faced a serious gas crisis.

Moscow's reaction to the disclosure of the scandal involving acts of state terrorism carried out by Russia on the territory of the Czech Republic in 2014, and to the expulsion of Russian spies by Poland and the Baltic states in 2021, was putting Poland, the Czech Republic, Lithuania, Latvia and Estonia on the Russian list of enemy countries. This case confirms that Russia is not interested in peaceful partnership with the region.

Russian hybrid wars

The Russian Federation vastly uses all elements of modern hybrid war, which are integrated with its diplomacy and economy. During Russian invasions in Georgia in 2008, and Ukraine in 2014, its conventional warfare was integrated with tactics such as covert operations and cyberattacks. Hybrid warfare - a strategy that employs conventional military force supported by irregular and cyber warfare tactics is used by the Kremlin against the NATO members. It is important to know that article 5 of the NATO treaty provides that if a NATO ally is the victim of an armed attack, each member of the Alliance will consider this act of violence as an armed attack against all members and will take the actions it deems necessary to assist the Ally attacked. It means all hybrid war tactics e.g. fake news, diplomacy, lawfare and foreign electoral intervention are below the article 5, and this kind of aggression against a NATO member may not obliged other members to help the victim of such aggression.

Training, exercises and education play a significant role in preparing to counter hybrid threats. The 3SI countries should exercise together in decision–making processes and joint military and non-military responses. Especially that the hybrid war activities are often focus on important parts of state economy (infrastructure, natural resources).

Russian resources and 3SI
Russia has the 8th biggest reserves of oil in the world (80 billion barrels), is the second biggest producer of oil (9.865 barrels per day), and number 5 in the world in terms of oil consumption (3.693 barrels per day). Over 9% of Russian Gross Domestic Product (GDP) comes from oil.
Russia is also important natural gas producer (no. 2 in the world – 22.7 billion MMcf in 2019, compare to Romania (no.

48 – 403 million), and Poland (no. 54 – 217 million). More than 24% of world gas reserves are in Russia.

Except oil and gas, the Russian Federation has vast amount of other minerals, e.g. Russia is no. 3 in the world in the production of gold (311 tons in 2019, compare to Bulgaria – 9.5 tons, and Poland 2.6 tons); in the production of silver it is no. 4 in the world (2.040 metric tons in 2018), compare to Poland (1.471 tons), and Bulgaria (41.6 tons). Russia produced 22 tons of platinum in 2018 (no. 2 producer in the world); was no. 5 producer of iron in the world, no. 8 producer of copper (Poland no. 13, Bulgaria no. 24); Russia is also no. 2 in the world in the production of cobalt.

Europe imports from Russia around 35%-40% of natural gas, which is transported and controlled by the Russian state-owned company Gazprom. The majority of that comes through pipelines which goes through Belarus and Poland to Germany, Nord Stream, which goes directly to Germany on the bottom of the Baltic Sea, and pipelines that go through Ukraine.

North Macedonia, Moldova, and Bosnia imported 100% of gas from Russia (2019), Finland 90% (2020). The 3SI states also depend on Russian gas: Estonia, Latvia, Lithuania and Slovakia – 100%, Bulgaria 97%, Hungary 83%, Slovenia 72%, Czechia 63%, Austria 62%, Poland 57%.

There was a significant number of issues over the Russian gas prices including pipeline shutdowns, and diversify of energy sources is now a priority not only for the 3SI states but for all European Union.

According to Eurostat, around one third of the EU's petroleum oil imports came from Russia. For some countries such as Estonia, Poland, Slovakia and Finland, it's more than 75% of their imports of petroleum oils. Russia is the third-largest producer of oil worldwide, accounting for over 12% of global crude oil production.

The biggest and richest firms in Russia are oil and gas producers, according to statista.com: Gazprom ($68 billion by market capitalisation in 2020), Rosneft ($63 billion), Novatek ($52 billion), Lukoil ($49 billion, no. 10 among oil firms in the world), Gazprom Neft ($20 billion). These firms keep Russian Federation running.

The biggest and richest oil and gas firms in the 3SI are also very important parts of national economies: PKN Orlen (a Polish state oil refiner and petrol retailer - $8 billion by market capitalisation), MOL Group (a Hungarian multinational oil and gas company - $9 billion), PGNiG (a Polish state-controlled oil and gas company - $7 billion).

According to Stanford Bernstein Europe will need to invest $200 billion to diversify its imports of gas and oil, and final finish its dependency from Russian energy resources. It is even more difficult in the situation when Germany decided to close all its nuclear and coal-fired power plants, and is opposed to the extraction of shale gas, which is more expensive to extract but the 3SI states have its huge amount.

Gas and oil can be possibly imported to the 3SI states from Africa, the Middle East, and the Caspian Sea region. Energy resources from these directions are big enough to cover 50%-60% of Europe's needs but actually the EU countries don't cooperate on such important matter. The 3SI seems to be ideal forum to create one efficient strategy regarding energy resources that could be implemented to all Europe. It is not only about avoiding energy blackmails from Russia but also about cheap energy for the 3SI enterprises, which increase their profits and competitiveness. Russian exported to the 3SI countries in 2020 goods and services for $33 billion (imported for $19 billion), including overpriced oil and gas for over $20 billion. With diversified portfolio the 3SI states could save at least $5 billion each year in average on imports of energy resources.

Mentioned before Nord Stream gas pipeline, Friendship oil pipeline, and Turkish Stream gas pipeline are three Russian projects in Europe that have direct impact on the 3SI economies.

The Nord Stream is a system of offshore natural gas pipelines, running under the Baltic Sea from Russia to Germany, avoiding central Europe countries, with two pipelines running from Vyborg to Lubmin near Greifswald and two further pipelines running from Ust-Luga to Lubmin called Nord Stream 2. In Lubmin Nord Stream connects to the OPAL pipeline to Olbernhau on the Czech border and to the NEL pipeline to Rehden near Bremen. Nord Stream 1 has a total annual capacity of 55 billion m3 of gas, and Nord Stream 2 is expected to double this capacity to a total of 110 billion m3. The USA, Ukraine, and some 3SI states opposed Nord Stream, as the pipelines clearly increase Russia's influence in central Europe, and Russia can use them to blackmail Europeans – supply of Russian gas to such countries as Ukraine or Slovakia can be stopped any time without affecting gas supply to the German clients. Moreover, Germany pay the lowest prices in Europe for the Russian gas, and can re-sell it to other countries gaining additional profits. For example, German chemical firms which costs of production depend on cheap gas, can generate higher profits in comparison to their counterparts from other European countries. If Nord Stream 2 becomes the main gas transmission route to Europe, Germany and Russia will benefit, and the 3SI states will pay the bill.

The Friendship Pipeline is the world's longest oil pipeline and one of the biggest oil pipeline networks in the world. It carries oil some 4.000 kilometres from the eastern part of European Russia to points in Ukraine, Belarus, Poland, Hungary, Slovakia, the Czech Republic and Germany. The network also branches out into numerous pipelines to deliver oil throughout Europe.

According to statista.com Poland spent $4.2 billion on Russian oil in 2020, and Slovakia $1.5 billion.

The Turkish Stream (TurkStream) is a natural gas pipeline running from Anapa in Russia, crossing the Black Sea to the terminal at Kıyıköy in Turkey. It has two lines with a total capacity of 31.5 billion m3 of natural gas. The first line supplies Russian gas to Turkey and the second line transport natural gas to the 3SI countries: Romania and Bulgaria. From geopolitical perspective it is similar to the Nord Stream projects: Russia's goal is to influence a strategic partner – Turkey – that similarly to Germany can get cheap gas, and re-sell it to other countries. Russia wants to gain political favours from Germany and Turkey, and simultaneously break coherence of NATO.

Russia vs China

China became an important factor in the geopolitical relations between the 3SI countries and Russia. Moscow cannot ignore the fact that a powerful neighbour rose near its Asian borders. A big chunk of Russian resources have to be used in the Far East to watch that growing power. Those resources (espionage, military, diplomacy, cyber, media), cannot be used simultaneously in Europe.

The 16+1 initiative (Chinese equivalent to the 3SI) does not meet anybody's expectations so far, and it's difficult to predict its future impact on the triangle the 3SI, Russia, and China. Russian-Chinese temporary strategic partnership can be considered as the main reason of the 16+1 failure. Central

Europe is an American ally, and this can reduce Russian (and also Chinese) business activities in the region, but it should not be a reason to stop investments and trade.

Russia has allowed Chinese Huawei to participate in its 5G networks, taking the risk of giving China too much technological leverage. There is also a collaboration between these two powers on multitude projects in defence, e.g. advanced fighters, and early warning systems, which could be used against the 3SI countries. China showed lack of interest in the Russian aggression on Ukraine and Georgia, and most likely we should not expect any reaction from Beijing against Russia in the case any hybrid war actions in the 3SI states.

Russia vs Germany

The 3SI countries leaders not only need to plan their cooperation with Russia and Germany, but also they must consider any kind of collaboration between these two powers. The contemporary strategic Russian-German partnership has begun in 1990s, becoming very intensive after year 2000. It seemed to be based on a chancellor Bismarck's policy (from the XIX century) of keeping friendly relations with Russia to prevent two-front war (or any kind of confrontation) in the future.

Germans and Russians fought together against Napoleon, they both divided Poland between themselves, signed the Rapallo pact against the western powers in 1920s. Hitler started the Second World War in the alliance with Stalin in 1939, then attacked the Soviet Union in 1941 losing the war four years later. Germany continuously offered the Russia of both Yeltsin and Putin close partnership and extensive cooperation.

Considering historical facts both Russia and Germany are not particularly interested in Central Europe as a flourishing region, specially they are against the concept of twelve independent states with strong, competitive economies, supported by external powers such as USA or China.

What Russia & Germany want from the 3SI:
- They want the 3SI countries to follow their instructions;
- They want them to import German cars and Russian oil & gas;

What Russia & Germany don't want from the 3SI:
- They don't need the 3SI for anything;
- They don't want the 3SI to expand to Ukraine and Belarus;

What the 3SI want from Russia & Germany:
- To leave them alone;
- To establish profitable trade for all parties;

What the 3SI don't want from Russia & Germany:
- They don't want to be dependent on the Russian oil & gas;
- They don't want European super-state led by Germany;

Transport, Energy, Digital
Digital economy is a very interesting field of competition between the 3SI and Russia. On one side central Europe received western technologies in last thirty years, and the 3SI states modernised their industries to a good level, but the negative result of that is the fact that majority of best firms in the region belong to western corporations. Meantime, Russia enjoyed much less technological transfers and with its limited resources had to modernise first only the most important sectors of economy: military, media, gas and oil production and infrastructure. Advanced in times of the Soviet Union Space industry, became less competitive in comparison to

China and the USA. Russia was able to modernised its army after year 2008 much further than any of the 3SI countries, e.g. developing hypersonic missiles. Russian media sector is also very modern: Russia Today tv network provides its content in English, Spanish, French, German, Arabic, and Russian. RT has $300 million annual budget (France24 - $100 million), and brings the Russian view on global news. There are also several big tech firms based in Moscow: Yandex, Mail.ru, and Kaspersky anti-virus.

The 3SI countries have more R&D centers, more specialists, and more resources than Russia in digital (high-tech) sector, and the Initiative is the right forum to develop this kind of comparative advantage. It's really strange that there is no political decision so far to create an international tv network that would promote the 3SI states interests and values.

Software developers in central Europe are considered as ones of the best in the world. Thousands of talented programmers in the 3SI countries work for global IT corporations, own businesses, and participate in modernisation of national economies. Russia is known in the world from its dangerous cyberattacks, and ransom software. Central Europe can use its power in software development to challenge cyber Russia.

Conclusion & Recommendations

International trade has been always the best way of cooperation between countries but it can be sometimes used as a weapon in politics as Russia proved many times. There is a huge potential in terms of cooperation between Russia and the 3SI but Russia is the main source of instability, and possible future military invasion. Countries that lay further from the Russian borders are less concern about it than ones that have with Russia, but they still afraid of it. Waiting for the positive change on Kremlin and a democratic government in the biggest country in the world, the 3SI states have been developing relations with that country in culture, arts, and sports. Doing business in Russia? It's very risky today.

	Total Export	Total Import 2020	Russia to 3SI, 3SI to Russia	
Russia	$551 billion	$366 billion	$33 billion	5.99%
3SI	$977 billion	$966 billion	$19 billion	1.94%

	Area (km2)	Population	Nominal GDP, 2020	Nominal GDP per capita
Russia	17.130.000	144.100.000	1.7 tln	$11.654
3SI	1.219.000	111.163.000	2.1 tln	$18.650

Main pros and cons for the 3SI states from their cooperation with Russia:

ADVANTAGES	DISADVANTAGES
Culture, arts, and sports	Russia is a source of instability
	Hybrid wars & energy blackmails
	Nord Stream pact – a dangerous cooperation Germany - Russia

Part 3 - CENTRAL EUROPE - Historical background

Chapter 1 – Amber Road

Central Europe has always been an excellent place for trade. It spans from East to West, and (from) North to South of the continent, connecting trade routes that go as far as Asia and Africa. The Etruscan and Greek traders travelled to the heart of Europe long before Hungarians, Poles and Czechs had founded their countries, seeking precious goods such as fur, tin and amber to sell them later on the markets of Bagdad and Damascus.

The lands located among the three seas: The Baltic, Black and Adriatic ones are predestined to be reach, well populated and educated. Unfortunately, through centuries great dangers were coming to these lands from almost all directions, each time destroying civilisations and states built with so much pain on the banks of Danube, Vistula, Neman, and Dnieper rivers.

Black Sea's ports combined main European trade routes such as Amber Road with the major Asian trade routes such as the Silk Road, and indirectly with Via Maris (from Damascus to Heliopolis/Cairo). Adriatic Sea's ports (mainly Venice) connected central European Amber Road with all the Mediterranean, and further with the Trans Saharan trade. Baltic Sea's ports connected the region with Scandinavia and western Europe.

Not only were goods transported over these routes, but people also shared knowledge, ideas, and religious practices. Archaeologists discovered that the breast armament of the

Egyptian pharaoh Tutankhamen (XIV century before Christ) contains large Baltic amber beads.

The oldest known trade route in Central Europe was the Amber Road that went from ancient Rome and Venice to the Baltic Sea coast; through modern Slovenia, Hungary, Austria, Slovakia, Czech Republic, Poland, Lithuania, Latvia and Estonia. It mainly ran as other historic routes, through rivers' valleys.

In the period of the Roman Empire's heyday along with amber, other commodities such as honey, wax and animal skin and fur was exported to the Rome in exchange for Roman wine, gold, banquet dishes, textiles, brass, glass, tin and copper. Merchants and traders were protected by Roman military fortifications. The Amber Road joined the huge network of Roman roads connecting all parts of the Empire. Cities like Scarbantia (Sopron, Hungary) and Savaria (Szombathely, Hungary), Poetovium (Ptuj), Celeia (Celje), Calisia (Kalisz, Poland), and Emona (Ljubljana, Slovenia) were prospered along this road, multiplying their size and wealth.

The long range trade across the road was organised mainly by big Roman firms, which specialised in crafts and trade. Bankers, traders, workshops' owners and stallholders were following the Roman troops. They were selling to the soldiers food and items needed for everyday use, buying from them spoils of war.

Amber was one of the first items of long distance trade. It was light and of unique characteristics that made it worthwhile to transport it from the place where it was plentiful, the Baltic Sea area, to the places like the Mediterranean littoral where it was not. In some places such as the Samland of the south-eastern Baltic amber washes up onto the beach in basketful quantities. In ancient times the people of those areas were surprised that anyone would pay them for something that appeared to be available in limitless amounts. But to people outside of those areas amber was something of a beauty like no other substance. It could be used like a gem for decoration, but was light and warm unlike gem stones. Its other characteristics were also unusual. It could be set on fire and burned with the aroma of pine wood. At one stage in history the Germanic words for amber referred to this characteristic. It was called bernstein (burn stone).

The Greek, Thales of Miletus, discovered in about 600 B.C. that amber when rubbed with woollen cloth attracts small bits of things such as straw. The Arabic word for amber means literally straw robber. The Greek word for amber became the word for static electric phenomena. The English word amber, surprisingly derives from an Arabic word for whale anbar by way of late Latin and French. It is the same source as for ambergris (grey amber), another marine product found washed up on beaches.[14]

The local traders exchanged amber and other local products with foreign buyers, storing amber in ground pits, and furs in wooden buildings for later, in exchange for clasps for robes or belt fittings, or fabrics, bags of amber, beaver furs, leather, and wood. For better profit, merchants ventured far to the North, where the prices of Roman products rose. Difficulties in acquiring amber and the risk borne by merchant caravans reaching far away dictated a high price for this ore. Sometimes the price of an amber product was extremely high, it depended on the size of the processed raw material. In the lands that belonged to the Empire, the safety of travellers was supervised by the Roman authorities, while in the northern countries the authorities of tribes and tribal unions took care of it.

---

[14] www.sjsu.edu/faculty/watkins/amber.htm

For the Egyptians amber was "the tears of the eye of Ra, the sun god". The eye of Ra is most often connected with protection, divine justice, punishment and vengeance. Amber was also associated with the lioness goddess Sekhmet, daughter of Ra and one of his eyes. Small pieces of amber have been discovered inserted beneath the skin covering the hands of Egyptian mummies, in order to protect the dead in the afterlife. In the Greek mythology, amber was made from the tears of a nymph as they dropped into water or the tears that Apollo shed for his son Aesculapius. Heinrich Schliemann found amber beads in Troy, and in cupola tombs of Mycenaean culture built on Crete Island from ca. 1600 B.C.E.[15] The places of long-distance trade where Roman products were delivered from further parts of the Empire, and exported to Pannonia (today's Hungary), were urban centres located at the intersections of the main communication routes, right next to the legionary camps. In addition to trading places surrounded by halls, there were also postal and customs stations. In these places, Roman goods were distributed for the northern peoples.

Gaius Plinius Secundus – Roman historian from the first century AD – wrote about an expedition to the Baltic Sea made by Caesar Nero's officials who brought great amount of amber used to celebrate gladiators' fights. The Romans valued amber both as medicine and for decorative purposes.

Studying ancient maps of Europe we may ask a question why the Romans did not conquered vast lands of Central and Eastern Europe, that belong today to Ukraine, Poland or Estonia. Maybe they did not like the local climate? Or there

---

[15] waughfamily.ca/Ancient/Amber%20in%20the%20Ancient%20Near%20East%20_%20Graciela%20Gestoso%20Singer%20-%20Academia.edu.pdf

was nothing to conquer expect never ending forests? The Germanic tribes in the north and north-east of Europe presented serious threat to the Roman Empire's borders. The Romans appeared to have attempted to conquer present-day Germany and establish a Roman province there. This ended in disaster for them at the Battle of the Teutoberg Forest in 9 AD when an alliance of Germanic peoples ambushed Roman legions and their auxiliaries.

The Romans under Marcus Aurelius launched the Marcomannic Wars (German and Sarmatian Wars) between 166 - 180 AD, in an attempt to extend Roman control in central Europe over areas of today's Hungary, Slovakia, and Czechia. The wars were brought to a halt with Emperor Aurelius's death in 180 AD. Most likely conquering Central and Eastern Europe would be too expensive and not worth of that similarly to conquering today's Scotland. The Roman strategic goal was to conquer all lands around the Mediterranean. The great plains of Eastern Europe had soils too tough for farming before the invention of improved plows during the Middle Ages. Though some places like the Crimea was early settled and farmed, the interior remained a place where various groups of people without fixed habitation regularly moved to different areas. Usually they were hunter-gatherers, pastoral nomads, tinkers and trader nomads. So the Romans preferred to extend their borders in directions of the Middle East and Egypt where the benefits to control usually settle large populations exceeded costs. The Mediterranean was a "sea highway" that was used by Rome for cheap and fast transport of goods (e.g. grain from Egypt, silver from Spain). Even more important than gold from the trade were Roman legions, that had to be moved quickly across the empire to stop any threats from neighbouring states or to deal with numerous rebellions in Roman provinces. The internal sea

(Mediterranean) was "surrounded" by thousands kilometres of Roman roads. For instance, Rome had between 25 to 30 legions (5.000 solders each) and from the time of general Gaius Marius onwards, legionaries received 225 denarii a year (a denarius was a Roman silver coin); this basic rate remained unchanged until Domitian, who increased it to 300 denarii. So a 100 denarius represents a 100 days of an agricultural worker who would have worked for 12 hours each day, or approximately £4.100 in modern money. Keeping three legions in Pannonia cost around 4.5 million denarii that was collected from the province.

Similar situation was with the Greeks and Alexander the Great who conquered Asia Minor, Egypt and the Middle East up to India as those lands were reach and prosperous. Alexander never considered to conquer the Balkan or the Danube's lands as it would be too much hassle and little benefits. However, the Greeks penetrated coasts of the Adriatic and Black seas establishing numerous trade routes, towns and ports: Adria, Salona, Odessos, Tomis, Tyras, Olbia, Fanagoria, Tanais. A Greek legend says that Jason and the Argonauts set out over the Black Sea to find the Golden Fleece in the land of Colchis (present-day Georgia). The Roman Empire took over some Greek colonies on the Black Sea coasts but never controlled the whole sea as they were more interested in the Oriental trade routes (e.g. from the Nile to the Red Sea, not across central Asia).

Two Roman provinces in central Europe played an important role in terms of trade between the Adriatic and the Black Sea: Pannonia - the territory west of the Danube (conquered between 35 - 9 BC), present-day western Hungary, eastern Austria and northern Slovenia and Croatia, and Dacia – annexed by emperor Trajan in 106 AD, present-day Hungary and Romania. Transforming Dacia into a province was a very resource-intensive process. Traditional Roman methods were employed, including the creation of urban infrastructure such as Roman baths, forums and temples, the establishment of Roman roads, and the creation of colonies composed of retired soldiers. However, excluding Trajan's attempts to encourage colonists to move into the new province, the imperial government did hardly anything to promote resettlement from existing provinces into Dacia.[16]

Dacia was an important producer of wheat, was linked into Rome's monetary economy (bronze Roman coinage was produced there), new Roman roads throughout the province facilitated economic growth. Local gold mines attracted Dalmatian miners but over time gold reserves were exploited. Dacian salt, iron, silver, copper and building-stone materials were also exported to Rome. Bronze casting foundries, weapon smithies, and glass manufactories existed in Dacian towns. Villages continued to specialise in craftwork such as pottery.

Also Pannonia was equally productive. Roman emperors Probus and Galerius who reigned between 305-314 AD, ordered local great forests to be cleared which caused that timber became its most important export. After that large areas became available for farmers exploitation who mainly produced oats and barley, from which the local farmers brewed a beer, but also vines and olives. trees were little cultivated.

Amber Road has its continuance in contemporary Poland: a north-south motorway that runs from Gdańsk on the Baltic Sea to the Polish-Czech border and connects with the Czech motorway D1 is officially called Amber Highway. Poland is also

---

[16] Burns, Thomas S. (2003). Rome and the Barbarians: 100 B.C.-A.D. 400, p.103

a world power in the export of amber jewellery. It is estimated that over 70% of the world's amber jewellery comes from Poland. The annual turnover of this industry is approx. EUR 200 million.[17] Amber prices can range from £20 to £40,000 or more.

Chapter 2 – Christianity
(Post-Roman times, Early Middle Ages, From VI to XIII century, Tribes from central Europe move to the west, new, mainly Slavic tribes came from East and settle in Central and Eastern Europe, with time became Christianised)

By the end of fifth century the Roman Empire lost its strengths and collapsed. Political turmoil, cultural change, disease, and socioeconomic instability contributed to the unrest, as well as the invasion of Germanic barbarians during the Migration Period (c. 375-568, a time of widespread migration of and invasions by peoples within or into the Roman Empire). Antiquity has finished and the Middle Ages began in Europe. The victorious Roman legions were defeated, and did not protect trade connections with other parts of the world anymore, including those with Central and Eastern Europe. Roman civil administration based in thriving cities lost its effective control over public finances, production and trade.

In the chaos of post-Roman world, and the westward movement of Germanic tribes in the 5th and 6th centuries CE, the Slavs emerged in Eastern Europe in conjunction with the movement of Huns, and later Avars and Bulgars. The Slavic tribes started the great migration   settling the lands

---

[17] www.3cargo.com/polski-eksport-jakie-towary-wysylamy-za-granice/

abandoned by barbarian (mainly Germanic) tribes fleeing the Huns and their allies: westward into the country between the Oder and the Elbe-Saale line; southward into Bohemia, Moravia, much of present-day Austria, the Pannonian plain and the Balkans; and northward along the upper Dnieper river. Some Slavs migrated with the Vandals to the Iberian Peninsula and even North Africa.

An old legend refers to three Slavic brothers: Lech, Czech and Rus on a hunting trip, followed different prey and thus settled in different directions: Lech in the north, Czech in the west, and Rus in the East, establishing three new nations – Lechites (the Poles), the Czechs, and the Ruthenians (Ukrainians/Russians).

When Slavic peoples finished their migrations, their first states appeared, each one ruled by a prince with a treasury and defence forces. In the 7th century, the Frankish merchant Samo supported the Slavs against their Avar rulers and became the ruler of the first known Slav state in Central Europe, Samo's Empire which was the foundation for later West Slavic states. The oldest of them were Carantania, the Principality of Nitra, Great Moravia and the Balaton Principality. The First Bulgarian Empire was founded in 681 as an alliance between the ruling Bulgars and the local Slavs, and their South Slavic language, the Old Church Slavonic, became the main and official language of the empire in 864. Bulgaria was influential in the spread of Slavic literacy and Christianity to the rest of the Slavic world. The expansion of the Magyars (Hungarians) into the Carpathian Basin and the Germanization of Austria gradually separated the South Slavs from the West and East Slavs. Later Slavic states, which formed in the following centuries, included the Kievan Rus (today's Ukraine), the Kingdom of Poland, Duchy of Bohemia, the Kingdom of Croatia, Banate of Bosnia and the Serbian Empire.

The West Slavs came under the influence of the Western Roman Empire (Latin) and of the Catholic Church.

The East Slavs came particularly under the influence of the Byzantine Empire and of the Eastern Orthodox Church.

The South Slavs (except the Slovenes and Croats) came under the cultural sphere of the Byzantine Empire, and of the Eastern Orthodox Church, while the Slovenes and the Croats were influenced by the Western Roman Empire (Latin) and thus by the Catholic Church.

Some major nations in Central and Eastern Europe are not Slavic origin: Hungarians, Romanians, Lithuanians, Latvians and Estonians.

The pagan Central and Eastern Europe populations were Christianised between the 7th and 12th centuries. While the spread of Christianity in those countries took centuries to finish, the process was ultimately successful, as within several decades they joined the rank of established European states recognised by the papacy, the Byzantine Emperor and other rules of European powers. The baptismal missions usually began in the major cities, where rulers were baptised first, then upper classes of the society and plebs at the end.

The Christians were persecuted in the Roman Empire for three centuries till 313 AD when the emperor Constantine the Great granted Christianity legal status, and then in 380 AD, the emperor Theodosius made Christianity the official religion of the Roman Empire. However, Rome did not become Christianised overnight, changing its beliefs slowly over time.

In 285 AD, Emperor Diocletian divided the Empire into two parts (his Empire was too big to manage), the Eastern Roman Empire (also called Byzantium, Constantinople) and the Western Roman Empire. When the Western Roman Empire fell in 476 AD, Christianity was still spreading. It is also important to remember that Christianity itself did not appear suddenly or fully-formed. Christianity grew out of Jewish traditions and was shaped by Roman cultural and political structures for several centuries. A few centuries later, in 1054 Christianity split in two branches: Eastern Orthodox Catholics (Byzantium) and Roman Catholics. The split happened when in Central and Eastern Europe new countries were forming and they were Christianised in both ways: from Rome or from Constantinople.

In adopting Christianity as the state religion, Central and Eastern European rulers sought to achieve several personal goals. It was a way of strengthening their hold on power, as well as using it as a unifying force for their people. New religion replaced several smaller cults with a single, central one, clearly associated with the royal court. It usually improved the position and respectability of the states on the international scene. The Church also helped to strengthen the monarchs' authority and brought to new Christian countries much experience with regard to state administration. Thus, the Church organisation supported the state, and in return, bishops received important government titles (e.g. in Poland with time, they became members of the Senate).

Great Moravia

Great Moravia was the first West Slavic major state that was mainly to emerge in the area of Central Europe, which are parts of today's Czechia, Slovakia, Poland, Hungary and Serbia. Moravia experienced significant cultural development under King Rastislav, when in 863 the mission of Saints Cyril and Methodius (Greeks from Thessaloniki) arrived from Byzantine introducing literacy (Glagolitic alphabet), Slavonic liturgy and a legal system.

Later, the saints were expelled from Great Moravia and the country changed its orientation to Western Christianity but they had a significant impact on other Slavic countries: in the Bulgarian Empire the Glagolitic script was substituted by Cyrillic which used some of its letters. The Cyrillic script and translations of the liturgy were disseminated in the Balkans and Kievan Rus, influencing Slavic cultural development and establishing the Cyrillic alphabets on territories of today's Belarus, Bosnia, Montenegro, North Macedonia, Russia, Serbia, and Ukraine.

Vikings
In IX and X centuries Central and Eastern Europe experienced Vikings' invasions.
They were people from today's Denmark, Norway, and Sweden who were not only warriors but also settlers and explorers. These explorations and settlements have had a decisive impact upon many places in Europe that persists even today. They were driven by political ambitions, the desire for wealth through tribute, engaging in trade, piracy, and mercenary activities.
They migrated eastwards and southwards through what is now Russia, Belarus, and Ukraine, roamed the river systems (Volga and Dnieper Rivers), reaching both the Black and the Caspian Seas, and Constantinople. Scandinavian settlements were also set up along the southern coast of the Baltic Sea, mainly for trade purposes. They were larger than the early Slavic ones, their craftsmen had a considerably higher productivity, and were capable of seafaring. However, their trade with the Slavic world was limited to the coastal regions and their hinterlands.
The Baltic Sea became a place of rivalry between Slavic and Viking pirates during that period; the Wolin and Rugen islands were centers of Slavdom, and also a place of much interaction with the Scandinavians. While Vikings raided lands in Poland,

Lithuania, and Latvia, Slavs also raided Scandinavia. The Wends, a Slavic people in modern day Eastern Germany, raided and pillaged much of Denmark. Viking mercenaries served for early Polish princes and fought against other Scandinavians serving in Kievan Rus.

An important reason why the Vikings travelled eastwards, was their desire to establish trading connections with the Byzantine Empire. Its capital Constantinople – today's Istanbul – was the trading centre for goods from the whole of the Mediterranean region, North Africa and the Near East. Here Vikings could buy exotic products such as silk, embroidered cloth, wine, fruit, spices, as well as semi-precious stones like carnelian and quartz. There was demand for these goods in the Scandinavian market. The long and difficult transport routes made them even more valuable when they finally reached the trading towns of Birka, Kaupang and Hedeby.[18]

The Vikings raids stopped somewhere in the XI century but had a significant impact on nations in Central and Eastern Europe, improving their skills and knowledge in sailing, weaponry and city building.

Bulgarian Empire

Between VIII and IX century the Bulgarian Empire expanded vastly its territory, covering today's Serbia, North Macedonia, Greece, Romania and Moldova and became one of the major powers in Europe. In 864 Bulgaria adopted Christianity from the neighbouring Byzantium. The Byzantine Empire saw in Bulgaria a serious threat after numerous military campaigns that the Bulgars successfully conducted. Byzantine emperors challenged the new regional power and after endless wars

---

[18] en.natmus.dk/historical-knowledge/denmark/prehistoric-period-until-1050-ad/the-viking-age/expeditions-and-raids/dangerous-journeys-to-eastern-europe-and-russia/

Bulgaria's strength was exhausted. In 1018 Bulgaria lost several important battles and ultimately became a Byzantine province.

In 1205 Bulgaria became a regional power again spreading from the Adriatic to the Black Sea. In the late XIII century, the Bulgarian Empire declined under constant invasions by the Mongols, Byzantines, Hungarians, and Serbs. In 1396 Bulgaria joined the Crusade of the Hungarian king Sigismund against the Turks but the Christian army was defeated in the battle of Nicopolis, and the Muslim invaders brought an end to the medieval Bulgarian state.

In the Early Middle Ages exchange of goods became occasional, and ancient long-range trade routes disappeared. Cities, towns and villages became almost entirely self-efficient. Farmers had difficulties to sell their agriculture products, and because of that they did not have enough money to buy tools and items for their homes. There was general lack of safe roads and travelling was impossible due to hard natural terrains such as forests, swamps, and lakes.

Gold and golden coins became a rare form of payments. Local trade was dominated by barter and when exchanging products was not possible, traders used salt, silver and pieces of canvas instead.

Hansa

The Hanseatic league (Hansa), was a commercial and defensive confederation of merchant guilds and market towns in Northwestern and Central Europe. Growing from a few North German towns in the late 1100s, the league came to dominate Baltic maritime trade for three centuries along the coasts of Northern Europe. Hansa territories stretched from the Baltic to the North Sea and inland during the Late Middle

Ages, and diminished slowly after 1450. Merchants established the league to protect the guilds' economic interests and diplomatic privileges in their affiliated cities, as well as along the trade routes which the merchants used. The Hanseatic cities had their own legal system and operated their own armies for mutual protection and aid. Despite this, the organization was not a state, nor could it be called a confederation of city-states.

The principle city of Hansa was German Lubeck that provided access for trade with Scandinavia and Kievan Rus putting it in direct competition with the Scandinavian traders who had previously controlled most of the Baltic trade-routes. Over the time, a network of Hansa's cities grew to about 170, including London (its Kontor stood west of London Bridge near Upper Thames Street, on the site now occupied by Cannon Street station), Brugge, Gent, Hamburg, Kopenhagen, Gdańsk, Elbląg, Klaipeda, Riga and Tallin.

The league primarily traded timber, furs, resin (or tar), flax, honey, wheat, and rye from the east to Flanders and England with cloth and manufactured goods going in the other direction. Metal ore such as copper and iron, and herring came southwards from Sweden.

German colonists in the 12th and 13th centuries settled in numerous cities on and near the east Baltic coast, which became members of the Hanseatic League, and some of which still retain many Hansa buildings and bear the style of their Hanseatic days. Most were granted Lübeck law, after the league's most prominent town. The law provided that they had to appeal in all legal matters to Lübeck's city council.

As an essential part of protecting their investment in ships and their cargoes, Hansa trained pilots, erected lighthouses and also waged a vigorous campaign against pirates. Hansa's ship travelled in convoys which was helping to deal with pirates.

Hansa became the main intermediary connecting goods exchange between Central and Western Europe, controlling trade routes on both Baltic and North Seas and also rivers that flew to these seas. It was promoting ship development and was introducing new rules and bans regarding the sea transport. In the pick its expansion, Hansa had over one thousand ships, and to achieve its monopoly Hanseatic cities were not allowed to sell ships to those who were not the members of the league. Its powerful navy defeated the Denmark's fleet in 1370 gaining 15% of profits from the Danish trade.

Between 1392 and 1440 maritime trade of the league faced danger from raids of the Victual Brothers and their descendants, privateers hired in 1392 by Albert of Mecklenburg, King of Sweden, against Margaret I, Queen of Denmark. In the Dutch–Hanseatic War (1438–1441), the merchants of Amsterdam sought and eventually won free access to the Baltic and broke the Hanseatic monopoly.

The Teutonic Order

In 1226 Polish Duke Konrad I of Masovia brought the Teutonic Order Knights from Palestine intended to Christianise the Baltic Old Prussians. The Knights (who were basically the Germans) had quickly taken steps against their Polish hosts and with the German Emperor's support, had changed the status of Chełmno Land, where they were invited by the Polish prince, into their own property. Following that, the Order created the State of the Teutonic Knights, expanding its borders by the conquered Prussians' territory, and subsequently conquered Livonia. In the next two centuries, this new German state on the Baltic coast became a major threat for the kings of Poland.

The Teutonic Order was founded in 1190 in the Holy Land as a military-monastic order that, following its defeat in crusades against the Arabs was looking for an opportunity to come back to Europe. Before the Order accepted Duke Konrad's invitation, they were invited by the Hungarian king Andrew II, who offered the Order a land in eastern part of his country to tackle constant attacks from pagan nomads. The Teutonic Knights built castles there and gained a pope's recognition that area as their property. The Hungarian monarch opposed such situation and expelled the Order, which saved Hungary from many future troubles. The same year Prince Konrad of Mazovia invited the Order to help protect Christian Poland's northern borders against pagan tribes of Prussia. At the beginning of the XIII century, the Prussians, as well as the Lithuanians, were the last areas of paganism on the southern coast of the Baltic Sea.

In a few years the Order conquered Prussia, incorporated Livonia, and continued its expansion by the fire and the sword. Soon it occupied some Polish lands including Pomerania and Lithuanian Samogitia, which cut off both countries from the Baltic coast and limited their foreign trade.

The Mongols

In the XIII century, Central and Eastern Europe was invaded by the Mongols. After destroying principalities of today's Russia and Ukraine and burning the city of Kiev, in 1241 the Mongols attacked with three armies commanded by one of the most prominent Genghis Khan generals - Subutai. One army defeated in the battle of Legnica the Polish forces led by Henry II, Duke of Silesia. A second army crossed the Carpathian mountains and the third one followed the Danube river. Then, the combined armies crushed Hungary at the Battle of Mohi. Mongols killed half of Hungary's population and the following year extended their control into Austria and Dalmatia, then invading Moravia.

The invaders from Asia started thinking about the conquest of Western Europe states.

But than a real miracle happened. General Sabutai and all the "Princes of the Blood" (of Genghis Khan) were recalled to Mongolia upon the death of Ögedei Khan to elect the new Khan.

To the Mongols, the European invasions were a third theatre of operations, second to both the Middle East and Song China. The Mongol incursions into Europe helped to draw attention to the world beyond the European space, especially China, which actually became more accessible for trade as long as the Mongol Empire itself lasted since the Silk Road was protected and secure. To some extent, the Mongol Empire and the Mongol invasion of Europe served as a bridge between different cultural worlds[19].

After almost two decades of civil wars in the empire, the Mongols came back, invading Europe several times and destroying big parts of Lithuania, Poland, Hungary, and Bulgaria. However, these attacks were less devastating as the local rulers were much better prepared: their main cities gained more fortifications, generals learnt new tactics, armies gained new weapons, monarchs signed new alliances.

At their height, the rulers of the Mongol Empire conquered, occupied, and controlled an area of 9 million square miles. In comparison, the Roman Empire controlled 1.7 million sq mi, and the British Empire 13.7 million sq mi, nearly 1/4 of the world's landmass.[20]

---

[19] www.newworldencyclopedia.org/entry/Mongol_invasion_of_Europe

The Mongol conquest had a huge impact on all spheres of live in Europe. New trade routes were open after establishing the Mongol Empire, connecting Europe with China, India and the Middle East. Traders and explorers were able to travel along those routes for thousands of kilometres relatively safety (e.g. Marco Polo), exchanging goods, ideas, and knowledge. Local rulers, especially those on the Silk Road, built post stations, rest stops, introduced the use of paper money, and soon Chinese silk appeared on the Central European markets. The Mongols brought many Chinese inventions, unknown to the Europeans before, e.g. guns and gunpowder.

It also allowed a deadly disease – so called "black death" - to travel from western China and Mongolia to Europe along newly restored trade routes in XIV century that killed at least 50 millions of people: around 25% of population in some regions of Central and Eastern Europe, and between 50% - 60% in Western Europe.

---

[20] www.thoughtco.com/mongols-effect-on-europe-195621

Chapter 3 – Central Europe in XV century

1 - Beginning of the Polish-Lithuanian Commonwealth

The Polish–Lithuanian Commonwealth (also known as the Crown of the Kingdom of Poland and the Grand Duchy of Lithuania, Rzeczpospolita, the Commonwealth of Poland, often simplified as the Kingdom of Poland, or just Poland), was a federation of Poland and Lithuania ruled by kings in real union, who were both King of Poland and Grand Duke of Lithuania. It became one of the largest and most populous countries of 16th to 17th-century Europe. At its largest territorial extent, the Commonwealth (Rzeczpospolita) covered almost 1m square kilometres with population around 12 million.

The union was one of the longest-lasting political unions in European history, yet it is known more for the way it ended, destroyed by its neighbours in the late eighteenth century, than for its success in sustaining for over four centuries a consensual, decentralized, multinational, and religiously plural model of political union based on a concept of republican citizenship. From its inception in 1385–6, a vision of political union was developed that proved attractive to Poles, Lithuanians, Ruthenians, and Germans.[21]

At the end of XIV and beginning of XV century Lithuania was the largest territorially country in Europe, and the last pagan state, exposed to constant attacks by the Teutonic Order. Poland also had problems with the Teutonic Knights and the union with Lithuania opened the possibility of a strong military alliance, building a regional power, as well as

---

[21]www.worldcat.org/title/oxford-history-of-poland-lithuania-volume-1-the-making-of-the-polish-lithuanian-union-1385-1569/

Christianisation in eastern Europe, being baptised Lithuania joined the family of European countries, which also brought economic and cultural benefits.

Although the territory of the Grand Duchy of Lithuania was more than twice as large as Poland in 1385, it was less developed. Its area between the thirteenth century and the mid-fifteenth century increased tenfold, encompassing the territories of many cultures, religions and peoples, among which the Lithuanians constituted a definite minority. In the second half of the fourteenth century, a conflict with Moscow became another growing threat, while in the west, Lithuania was still under attack by the Teutonic Knights, and simultaneously being also consumed by internal conflicts, which was influenced by the principle of inheriting the prince's throne by all male heirs. The union was guaranteed by the Polish nobility and Lithuanian boyars, which made it a union of two sovereign states.

From 1413 the Polish part of the new state organism was called the Crown, and the Lithuanian part - the Grand Duchy of Lithuania.

The equality of the Lithuanian and Polish sides was emphasised by extending the privileges of the Polish nobility to the Catholic Lithuanian boyars (50 boyar families was adopted to Polish noble coats of arms).

The union significantly increased the positions of both states in Europe. Before the unification, Lithuania as a pagan country, did not count at all in the European politics, and Poland was too weak to conduct foreign policy on a larger scale, for example to oppose the might of the Czechs. Thanks to the union, Lithuania maintained its statehood, threatened by Moscow and the Teutonic Knights entering the circle of Latin culture. The joint Polish-Lithuanian state became a significant power, and the largest state organism in Europe at that time. The culture of both countries also changed - on the one hand, Polish culture related to Western civilization emanated into Ruthenian and Lithuanian lands, on the other hand, eastern elements influenced Polish culture, which gave it a specific character.

2 – Noble democracy

One of the main results of that new culture in central Europe was the noble democracy, which beginning is considered to be the year 1454, when the land assemblies (congresses of local nobility), under the Nieszawa privileges, were granted broad powers in state affairs and participation in power. The new system introduced formal equality of all nobility, but the informal hierarchy has not disappeared. The magnates, although in a legal sense were not separated from the rest of the nobility, actually occupied a higher position than the average nobility. This, in turn, stood above the farm nobility and the naked nobility, i.e. those without land (non-owners). The land assemblies quickly gained in importance, and in the second half of the fifteenth century, they increasingly entered the sphere of government. The deputies delegated by the land sejmiks to the general parliament of the Kingdom of Poland soon created a separate chamber of deputies, and the Nihil Novi Constitution of 1505 approved the role of land deputies with equal rights in relation to noble senators. From then on, their consent was required to make new law.[22]

3 – The Jagiellonian dynasty

---

[22]   https://publicystyczny.pl/problemy-demokracja-demokracja-szlachecka-pierwszej-rzeczpospolitej/

The Union also introduced the Jagiellonian dynasty to the Polish throne, that ruled the country for almost two hundred years, and led to the flourishing of the state, and the "golden age" in its history. The tangible benefit of the union was the defeat of the military power of the Teutonic Order, which so far threatened both non-allied countries, and most importantly, gaining access to the Baltic Sea. Many historians argue that the Jagiellonian kings neglected Western Borderlands of the country in exchange for interest in the East and involvement in conflicts with Moscow and the Tatars (descendant of the Mongols).

From 8 to10% of the total population of the Rzeczpospolita were noblemen, thanks to which the noble democracy system had a broad social base for those times. The nobility with time reached such a strong position in the state that they were able not only to effectively oppose the magnates' interests, but also to formulate, implement and put forward their own reform program, known as the "Execution Movement".

4 – Novgorod Republic

In the context of Poland-Lithuania relationship it is necessary to mention here about its important ally – the Novgorod Republic. City of Veliky Novgorod was created in 1136 as a result of the division of the Grand Duchy of Kiev into the districts. It was a state with a specific form of democracy developed over time, where the assembly of the city's citizens, merchants and boyars, elected a mercenary ruler - the prince (that could also be remove by them).

In the years 1389-1392 and 1407-1412, the Novgorod Republic remained in a feudal relationship to the Kingdom of Poland, and its army took part in the Battle of Grunwald fighting against the Teutonic Knights. In 1478 it was conquered by Ivan III the Stern and incorporated into the Grand Duchy of Moscow. It never regained its independence in the next centuries becoming a part of Russia.

5 - Teutonic Order Knights

At the beginning of the XV century the Order continued its expansionistic politics, declaring war to Poland in 1409, invading its border lands, and destroying town and villages on the Polish side. Soon the Lithuanian troops entered Semigallia supporting a local uprising against the Order. The Knights tried to tear deadly threat as it was for it from Poland-Lithuania alliance. Their new Grand Master Ulrich von Jungingen decided to crash the growing power of Poland-Lithuania once for all and attack first. However, the Poles expected it and prepared well. In summer of the following year, the combined Poland-Lithuania forces began marching on the capital of the Teutonic Order – Malbork (Marienburg). In the half way the Polish-Lithuanian forces met the main Teutonic army. In the battle of Grunwald on 15th July 1410 the Teutonic Knights were completely defeated, the Grand Master and main Teutonic leaders were killed. The battle is called the last big battle of the Medieval Europe, where the Polish King led 39.000 men against 27.000 troops of the Grand Master. A few days after the battle, the Polish and Lithuanian forces surrounded the Teutonic capital in Marienburg (Malbork).
The peace treaty signed several months later, confirmed a decline of the Teutonic power and an increase of Rzeczpospolita as a regional power. However, in spite of the great victory it was not the last conflict between Rzeczpospolita and the Order.

In 1454 another war broke when Rzeczpospolita openly supported the Prussian Confederation – an organisation formed by a group of nobles and clergy who oppose the rule of the Teutonic Knights, and formally asked King Casimir IV Jagiellon, to incorporate Prussia into the Kingdom of Poland. According to Peace of Thorn (1411) which followed the Teutonic Knights' defeat in the Battle of Grunwald, the Teutonic Order had to pay high reparations to Poland. The monastic state imposed high taxes on the cities to raise the funds which caused great crises that lasted for about three decades. The Prussian lords from major cities organised themselves to oppose the rule of the order which resulted in a long war that ended in the defeat of the Teutonic Order in 1466. The Order lost control of Pomerania with city of Gdańsk, and its core territories became Royal Prussia - a province of Poland with some autonomy.

Poland regaining access to the Baltic Sea, full access to the Vistula river, and connected trade routes going to western Europe with those coming from the coasts of the Black Sea. The increased demand for raw materials in Europe in the second half of the XV century coincided with the increased possibility of deliveries from Poland, which contributed to the dizzying pace of trade development along the Vistula and a significant development of grain exports, which dominated the Polish economy in the following years[23].

As a result of the privileges obtained during the war and the temporary blocking of the trade route by Elbląg, Polish maritime trade concentrated in Gdańsk. The city retained the right of exclusive commercial brokerage from 1442, extending its privileges to the right to control shipping and collect taxes. Polish authority over the mouth of the Vistula River remained

---

[23] Davies N., God's Games, vol. 1, Kraków, 1996, p. 288-290

severely limited. Gdańsk's profits from exclusive trade intermediation enabled the city to develop, thanks to which it became the largest and richest city in Poland, maintaining multiculturalism and far-reaching independence[24].

6 - Polish-Hungarian Union

At the beginning of the XV century, kingdoms of Central Europe tried to strengthen their position in the region by seeking alliances with neighbouring states. Poland and Hungary had royal dynasties related to each other, with good interactions started in the previous century, what gave them a good starting point for negotiations. At congress of Visegrad in 1339 Hungarian and Polish monarchs decided that if Casimir III of Poland died without a son, the son of Charles I of Hungary, would be the King of Poland, which actually happened in 1370. The new ruler did not have a son and when his daughter took the Polish throne, many lords started question her rights, as according to the Visegrad's agreement only a man could be the legitimate monarch. In spite of that, she manged to be crowned in 1384, and the Polish lords started looking for a right candidate to be her husband in the rapidly changing international environment. In the situation when the Polish-Hungarian Union could not be continued after 12 years, they attention was focused on the Lithuanian Grand Duke Jogaila (Wladyslaw Jagiełło), who turned out to be one of the best kings in the entire Polish history.

The first Poland-Hungary Union (1370-1382) did not meet great expectations from the noblemen in both countries but in the XV century many lords and royal

---

[24] Davies N., God's Games, vol. 1, Kraków, 1996, p. 302-306

leaders were thinking about a new union, that would combine all kingdoms of central Europe. Wladyslaw III became the new king of Poland and Grand Duke of Lithuania in 1434, and six years later also accepted the crown of Hungary and Croatia, which forced him to mainly focus on the political situation in Balkans, especially on the growing threat from the Turkish Empire. He led a successful military campaign in 1443/44 winning several battles, which resulted in signing a very beneficial truce that forced Sultan Murad II to leave occupied Serbia and returning 24 previously conquered Danube castles.

In spite of that great success, the young king was persuaded by his advisors to continue fighting against the Muslim Ottomans. He won several battles but then he was defeated and killed in the Battle of Varna (Bulgaria) in 1444. The Ottoman army of 60.000 troops could have been defeated by the Christian army of 20.000 men if prepared properly. King Wladyslaw's army was composed mainly of Hungarian, Polish, Bohemian (Czech) and Wallachian (Romanian) forces, with a small number of Papal knights, Teutonic Knights, Bosnians, Croatians, Bulgarians, Lithuanians and Ruthenians.

His death had serious consequences for the whole region: The second personal union between Poland and Hungary lasted only four years (1440-44). What is worse, in 1453 the Turks conquered Constantinople, ending one-thousand-year-long history of Byzantium (Eastern Roman Empire), and continued its expansion on Balkans.

According to a Portuguese legend Wladyslaw survived the Battle of Varna and then journeyed in secrecy to the Holy Land. He became a knight of Saint Catharine of Mount Sinai and then he settled on Madeira. King Afonso V of Portugal granted him the lands in Madalena do Mar district of the Madeira Islands, for the rest of his life.

From the beginning of the XV century Ottoman Turks aimed the Balkans as their prime goal of expansion. In spite of defeats at the hands of Tamerlane (the Mongol Khan), internal bloody rivalry for the throne, the Turks were fighting Venice and Hungary. After the fall of Constantinople they could enter deeply into European continent, which began the golden age of the Ottoman Empire. In XV century the Turks conquered Serbia (1459), Albania (1479), the Crimean Khanate (1475), Bosnia (1463). They also planned to attack Rome. Their conquest was not always successful and if there was bigger cooperation among the Balkan nations, it could be certainly stopped, for example in 1462, Mehmed II was driven back by Wallachian prince Vlad III Dracula in Targoviste, and Stephen the Great of Moldavia defeated the army of the Ottomans at the Battle of Vaslui.

7 - Economy & Trade

There were huge changes in Central and Eastern Europe Economy in the XV century.

Trade was largely in the hands of the Hanseatic League (primarily in Central Europe and the North and Baltic Sea regions) and the Italian City Republics, most notably Venice and Genoa (primarily in the Mediterranean region). At the end of the 15th century, the focus of trading activity shifted to the Atlantic following the discovery of America and new sea routes to Asia.[25]

---

[25] https://www.diercke.com

Changes in the European economy and trade in the XV century started the process called Economic dualism (agrarian dualism), that was the phenomenon of diverging development paths of the European feudal economy. Basically, in the countries of Eastern Europe (east of the Elbe River) economy grew much faster than in Eastern Europe, and there were several reasons for that.

The first reason was the fact that the Ottoman Empire conquering Byzantium and the Middle East blocked the trade between Europe and Asia (especially lucrative trade with India and Persia). The merchants were desperate to find new trade routes to reach those lands. First who did it were Portuguese sailors such as Bartolomeu Dias who sailed around Africa, building trade posts on its coast. There were others who followed them, and in consequence new trade routes were established far away from central and Eastern Europe, and old trade roads to Constantinople, Venice and Crimea were not in use.

Until the fall of Constantinople, trade routes ran south-east through Podolia, towards the Odessa Bay, towards the mouth of the Danube, towards the Turkish straits and towards the country of Baghdish Abbasids, and earlier to the country of the Khazars. There was money, trade flourished, everything went around there, there was New York, Brussels, and all that made our ancestors confident that power, fame and a future awaited in these centers.[26]

The second factor was the situation of peasants. Farmers in the west were free, and could move between villages or to cities when they wanted. That was not possible in Eastern Europe, where peasants were not allowed to leave their villages.

---

[26] J. Bartosiak: "Przeszłość jest prologiem", p. 290

Commodity-money relations developed in the west of the continent, while in the east there was re-feudalisation, secondary serfdom and naturalization of the economy. The reasons were to be different trends in agriculture - the elimination of the personal and legal dependence of the peasant in the West in the absence of such processes in the East, and economic conditions - the great demand of the dynamically developing colonial countries for grain that could not be covered by domestic agriculture. This implied high grain prices and the profitability of its production for Eastern Europe. Agrarian dualism was to lead to faster development of cities and industry in Western Europe, to the weakening of the internal market and economic stagnation in Eastern Europe.

In Western Europe, we are dealing with the shrinking of the land cultivated by the feudal lord and the development of the land lease system in exchange for a monetary rent, the commodity nature of agricultural production and its specialisation. There is also a stratification of villages, the emergence of profitable farms and the decline of the weaker ones. The legal situation of peasants also improved due to the gradual disappearance of personal servitude, e.g. the right to leave the village, dependence on common courts.

In Eastern Europe, on the other hand, we observe farm management based on the principle: low investment expenditure, high consumption, enlargement of the area of land cultivated by the feudal and agricultural production, small rent as the main form of feudal benefits, personal serfdom of the peasants, which resulted in the ban on leaving the village by the peasant and the right of the master to judge the peasant. All this led to the fact that the peasant farm in Eastern Europe was reduced to the function of a food plot, reproduction of labour and livestock.

Systematic progress in production techniques was observed in central and eastern Europe's craftsmanship of the XV century. The use of hydropower has increased, manifested by the widespread use of water wheels. Water energy was used not only in mills, but water also moved saws in sawmills, grinding wheels, bellows in forges and ore roasting ovens, activated huge hammers, allowed sheet metal rolling and wire drawing. The reel was introduced for the first time in production, and new crafts such as papermaking and printing appeared. Gutenberg's invention of printing in 1440 influenced the development of education, and allowed the rapid transmission of new ideas, helping the Renaissance spread rapidly from its birthplace in Italy to the rest of Europe.

Significant transformations also took place in mining and metallurgy. The growing demand for minerals required an increase in extraction in existing mines or the establishment of new ones. Such undertakings required enormous capital, and these needs could only be met by merchant capital. An example of such a shift of merchant capital into production are the silver and lead mines near Olkusz (Poland). After the shallow underground deposits were exhausted, it became necessary to build shafts and tunnels. Only merchants could provide the funds. However, the silver and lead mines developed slowly. The salt mines made much more progress. The increase in production was related to the expansion and improvement of these mines.

Chapter 4 – Central Europe in XVI century

Prussian Tribute

In 1525 in Kraków took place a Prussian Tribute (homage) – a new state on the Baltic coast – Prussia (formerly German Teutonic Order Knights) signed a peace treaty with Rzeczpospolita, and its ruler Duke Albert Hohenzollern became a vassal of the Polish king.

The ceremony had a solemn setting. The royal throne was erected on a platform leaning against the wall of the town hall and covered with cloth. In the morning, King Zygmunt the Old and Queen Bona left Wawel with their children. Before them were the senate and the court, the queen was followed by the ladies of the court. The king stopped in the town hall, where he changed into a coronation costume, while the queen took her place in the window of one of the tenement houses by the market square. In the morning the king took his throne, and the ceremony began.

First, the envoys of prince Albrecht arrived, fell on their knees and asked for grace to be shown him and to grant Prussia a hereditary fief. Vice-chancellor Piotr Tomicki replied on behalf of the king. When Prince Albrecht heard a favourable response from the envoys, he, clad in armour, rode up to the market square, dismounted in front of the landing, went to the throne, knelt and thanked the king for the sending. Albrecht Hohenzollern secularized the Teutonic state without much opposition. Moreover, he adopted Lutheranism, and other religious brothers and many inhabitants of Duchy of Prussia followed in his footsteps. Prussia became the first Protestant principality in Europe.[27]

---

[27] https://www.historiaposzukaj.pl/wiedza,wydarzenia,203,hold_pruski_1525.html

Hungary

After taking Greece and Bulgaria the Ottomans captured main cities of Albania, Serbia and Bosnia. Then vassalised Wallachia (Romania) and attacked the Kingdom of Hungary.

In 1526 Hungarian King Ludwik II Jagiellonian was defeated by the Ottoman Muslims in the Battle of Mohács. The battle has huge consequences for the Balkan nations and the shape of Central Europe.

Hungary was divided in three parts: the middle part of it with Buda and Pest, became a Turkish province, Transylvania became a vassal state of the Turks, and the western part with Croatia and Slovenia was ruled by Hungarian kings from the Austrian Habsburg dynasty.

The Union of Lublin

The Union of Lublin in 1569 transform the Polish-Lithuanian Commonwealth from a personal union into a real union, which means the Rzeczpospolita became one country ruled by a single elected monarch who carried out the duties of King of Poland and Grand Duke of Lithuania, and was governed with Senate and parliament (the Sejm). Now the state had also the same coat of arms, currency, foreign and defence policy – but still separate treasury, offices, army and judiciary.

The idea of permanent regulation of Polish-Lithuanian affairs and further integration developed throughout the 16th century. It resulted from changes in the internal situation of both countries, as well as from the international affairs.

When the Teutonic Order was finally defeated, one of the main pillars of the union from 1385 lost its importance. However, at the end of the XIV century, another power appeared that threatened the eastern borders of Lithuania. It was the increasingly powerful state of Moscow.

As early as 1473, the Grand Duke of Moscow, Ivan III, demanded that the Ruthenian lands belonging to the Lithuanian state, should be returned to him (despite the fact they had never belonged to Russia). A few years later, in 1484, he proclaimed himself the Tsar of All Russia, although this title was still used sporadically and unofficially (the first official coronation as tsar was performed by Ivan IV the Terrible in 1547). It all led to an open conflict. The first fights took place when Alexander Jagiellon held the grand-ducal throne in Vilnius. Their result was unfavourable for Lithuania, which lost a number of territories. The situation on the Eastern Front continued to worsen in the following years. In 1514, the key fortress of Smolensk was lost. Ten years before the conclusion of the Union of Lublin, the First Livonian War (1558) broke out between Poland and Lithuania on the one hand, and Moscow on the other. This conflict, like the previous ones, ended with the loss of significant areas of the principality. The threat posed by the Moscow state, which threatened Lithuania with losing its state, was not permanently removed. So it was a very important factor influencing the need to tighten Polish-Lithuanian relations, but not the only one.

The economic potential of the Polish-Lithuanian Commonwealth, especially in the field of food production, made it become "Europe's granary", gaining primacy among the wealthiest European countries at the end of the XVI century. The grain trade through the port of Gdańsk became the basis of the wealth of the nobility. Until the mid-XVII century, agricultural production continued to increase, peaking in 1628. However, with the increasing wealth of the nobility there was a slower growth of the cities and the total decline of the peasant class.

The Union of Lublin was also of great cultural importance. The Lithuanian and Ruthenian (Ukrainian and Belarusian) nobility adopted Polish and Western models, and Polish - Eastern and Oriental ones, which made the Polish-Lithuanian Commonwealth unique. The state thus became a bridge between East and West, an area of cultural exchange of unprecedented intensity.

Free elections

The last king from the Jagiellonian dynasty died in 1572 and from now on the following kings were chosen by parliament on free elections till the partitions of Poland in XVIII century.

Nobility created mechanisms that guaranteed that a new king would not violate their existing privileges, and they could gain some additional benefits at the same time.

The free elections were universal within the noble estate, and in fact it was free, as every nobleman could participate in it, and not only members of the parliament, as it was in the past. Around 50.000 noblemen arrived at the first free election but the next ones did not bring as many voters (at the second free election in 1575 only 12.000 of nobility).

The free election weakened the king's power, became a reason for disputes between voting provinces (disputes over candidates for the throne) and, above all, it gave the possibility for hostile countries to interfere with the Polish-Lithuanian state.

On 12 May 1575 Stefan I Batory (the Hungarian ruler of Transylvania) was chosen by the nobility as a new king. The monarch had ten counter-opponents in the election: a Graf of Prague, two voivodes, Duke of Ferrara, Ivan IV the Terrible and his son, king of Sweden, two Archdukes of Austria, and the emperor of Austria. Batory became the king only because the tsar and the emperor were unacceptable as candidates for the majority of noblemen and voted on him instead.

Polish fleet

Polish fleet on the Baltic Seas started growing when Rzeczpospolita regained Pomerania with Gdansk as a result of the won war against the Teutonic Order in 1466. It was basically the first war in the Polish history when combined military and naval operations helped to win. During that conflict the Polish privateer fleet, consisting mainly of Gdańsk ships blocked deliveries for the Order on the Sea, cutting it off from all supplies. At the same time the fleets of other Baltic states such as Sweden, and Denmark grew into power. The development of Polish navy was however slow. A Polish privateer fleet established in 1517 took part in two conflicts: the first was the Lithuanian-Moscow war (1512-1522), where Polish ships blocked the eastern Baltic, preventing the supply of weapons and equipment to the Grand Duchy of Moscow. The second was the Polish-Teutonic conflict in the years 1519-1521, when the Polish fleet again blocked Królewiec (Konigsberg).

The next stage in the development of the navy took place in the second half of the XVI century, when the Polish fleet numbered thirty ships. The Polish naval forces carried out the tasks of cutting enemy sea communication routes, which significantly influenced the course of military operations in Livonia. In 1558 the parliament (Sejm) established the Maritime Commission - the first in Poland and one of the first in Europe organs of state power at sea, that organised a privateer fleet, the first Polish professional maritime forces. Additionally, it supervised the construction of new units for the fleet. In the heyday of the Polish fleet, however, it was not without serious losses.

In 1571 the Danish fleet destroyed the Polish fleet on the Baltic Sea, and soon entered the waters of the Gulf of Gdańsk, sinking another two Polish ships that tried to take refuge in the coastal waters. Then the Danish fleet captured in the Bay of Puck 13 Polish ships and 5 ships, previously seized by the Poles hijacking them to Copenhagen, which was a devastating blow to the Polish navy. A few weeks later the Danes repeated the action but this time Polish fleet managed to hide in the port of Gdańsk, that did not meet Danish demands to hand over Rzeczpospolita's ships. Then the Danes blocked the port of Gdańsk intercepting and seizing over 50 Gdańsk merchant ships in the waters of the Baltic Sea. These events, however, did not prevent the further construction of military units.

Economy & Trade
Trade in the 16th century was marked in the history of Poland by the development of new routes and significant changes in the structure and quantity of exported and imported goods. Contacts with the Czech Republic and Hungary developed dynamically, which was caused by the episode of the Jagiellonian rule in those countries. Baltic trade was entirely monopolized by the Hanseatic League. It played an important role in the development of the Polish agricultural economy, creating demand for agricultural products and forest goods. Hanseatic ships transported grain, wood, hides, honey and wax from Poland, and they brought herring, salt and Flanders cloth. The increase in agricultural production intended for export in Poland has contributed to an increase in the role of the Vistula route and navigation on the Odra and Warta rivers.
The real union with Lithuania created new opportunities for Polish trade. Lithuanian lands have become a resource of

forest and agricultural products, and an outlet for iron products and staple products. Three new trade routes between Lithuania, and Poland began to take shape.

Important items of Polish exports were also wool, feathers and down. The internal markets were dominated by the grain trade fairs, local markets were thriving, and their role increased even more with time. Significant changes took place in the organisation of trade. Many marketplaces that were set in the Middle Ages turned out to be too tight and inhibiting for Polish trade. This mainly concerned the right to composition, which in the XVI century was abolished in almost all cities (except Gdańsk).

A new phenomenon in central European trade was the emergence of a group of bankers intermediating in credit operations in larger cities. Commercial companies specialising in the trade of one type of goods were also established, maintaining contacts with large department stores in Europe. The post office established by King Zygmunt August in 1558 played an important role in the development of trade.

Metallurgy developed also thanks to the mercantile capital. At the end of the 16th century, smelting furnaces appeared, enabling the melting of liquid iron and steel leveling. Despite this, central and eastern Europe was far behind the Western European steel industry. Forges, which were a separate social group with great privileges, dealt with metallurgical production. At the turn of the XVI and XVII centuries, the landowners began to buy hen-house plants and introduced forced labour, which had a negative impact on the further development of the Polish steel industry.

The mercantile capital went not only directly into production. Thanks to the entrepreneurship of Kraków merchants, a merchant and magnate company was established in 1525 to search for ores (mainly silver) in the Tatra Mountains.

The price revolution
In the first half of the XVI century, the prices of agricultural products began to rise rapidly in Europe (so called price revolution), while the prices of handicraft products stabilised at the same time. This phenomenon changed the income structure of rural and urban producers as a matter of the influx of precious metals from the New World, the development of urban areas, and the rapid increase in food demand.
The price revolution caused incomes with a fixed nominal amount to decline. This concerned the urban population and the landowners collecting fixed rents from peasants who sold food on the market and whose incomes grew. In order to prevent their incomes from falling, landowners switched to their own production, destined for the market, or undertook other forms of economic activity.
As long as the prices of agricultural produce continued to rise, the peasant in central and eastern Europe could afford to have helpers, produce his commodities for sale, and purchase goods produced in the cities. On the other hand, in Western Europe, with the personal freedom of the peasants and the predominance of leased farms, the countryside created a purchasing power for urban production, and simultaneously gave cities cheap labour.

Cities in XVI century
There were 689 cities in Poland at the beginning of the XVI century, 861 at the end of that century, and 929 in the mid of the XVII century. The number of cities increased by 25% in the XVI century, and only 8% in the first half of the XVII century

(the age of wars). The eastern borderlands of the Polish-Lithuanian Commonwealth, poorly urbanised in the Middle Ages, became an absorptive region for new settlement. Towns and cities constituting the centers of magnate latifundia and military fortifications grew rapidly creating the dense urban network in the mid-seventeenth century (one town per 255 km). In Volhynia and Podolia - less than 2 cities per 1000 km2, in Ukraine one city per 446 km2 (in 1625 there were 320 towns).

The settlement developed largely thanks to newcomers from Silesia and the Czech Republic, fleeing religious persecution. In Royal Prussia and Warmia in the XVI century, no new cities were established, because the great centers - Gdańsk, Elbląg, Toruń - did not agree to break their industrial and commercial monopoly.

Most likely around 25% of the country's population lived in cities at the end of the XVI century. The proportions for individual districts were different, from a few percent in the South-Eastern borderlands and a dozen or so in Mazovia to over 30% (Pomorze Małopolska, Wielkopolska). In absolute numbers, the estimates are imprecise, it is estimated that at that time in Wielkopolska, Małopolska and Mazovia had a total population of just over 600.000 to about 825.000 townspeople, the cities of royal Prussia had a population of just over 100.000. dwellings In the centers of the Grand Duchy of Lithuania, there lived about 560.000 population.

Small and very small towns (88%) prevailed in Korona. In the Grand Duchy of Lithuania, in the mid-17th century, Vilnius had a population of about 20,000 residents, and other cities had between 2 and 10 thousand (Grodno Troki Kaunas, Brest, Nowogródek, Minsk, Połock, Kiejdany, Kleck, Pińsk, Witebsk, Mohylów, Stary Bychów).

In Duchy of Prussia, connected with the fiefdom of the Republic of Poland, Królewiec was the most populous (over 10.000). In Livonia, over 10.000 people lived in Riga.

Cities were divided into royal (of the Commonwealth), private (noble or magnate) and church (diocesan or monastic). Distribution and pledges of the royal lands, significantly diminished the royal domain. King Sigismund I the Old released about 90 cities from pledges, Queen Bona bought about 15 cities in 1526, Mazovia brought about 35 to the royal treasury, pledges around 27 and bequests on estates partially exploited by the treasury was the cause of sharp opposition from the noble society. As a result of the opposition at the Sejm of 1550-155, referred to as the execution movement, King Sigismund II Augustus agreed to the property execution program. The pledges of royal estates from before 1504 were not subject to recovery, as they did not collide with the legal acts of 1440-1504.

Chapter 5 – Central Europe in XVII century

A Cossack rebellion on Ukraine
A Cossack rebellion took place between 1648 and 1657 in the eastern territories of the Polish–Lithuanian Commonwealth (present day Ukraine), which was triggered by cancelled preparations for a war with the Ottoman Empire. The sejm (parliament) opposed king's plans to prevent expected Turkish attack, and did not allow to collect additional taxes necessary for that. This upset the Cossack forces who were almost ready and expected great profits from the campaign against the Ottomans. Under the command of Hetman Bohdan Khmelnytsky, the Cossacks, in alliance with the

Crimean Tatars and local peasantry, fought against the Polish forces.

The Cossacks were free people of various origins (Ukrainian and Polish peasants, poor townspeople, petty nobility and ordinary adventurers), who from the end of the XV century lived near the lower Dnieper river, known as the Wild Fields. They were courageous people with a great sense of independence, prone to disobedience and rebellion, engaged in hunting, fishing and farming, who also liked military expeditions.

Polish kings highly respected the combat value of the Cossacks, especially the infantry, and incorporated some of them into military service. Such Cossacks were called registers, and were paid by the state for their service. There were many more willing to join the army to increase their social status.

At the beginning of 1654, a Russian emissary came to Kiev, and the rebelled Cossacks signed the settlement with Russia, which obligated them to obey the Tsar and recognise the supremacy of the Orthodox Church and accept the presence of the Russian garrison in Kiev. In return, the Cossacks had the right to elect Hetman, and keep an army of 60.000 troops. Upon the news of the Russian-Cossack alliance, the Crimean Khan decided to enter into an alliance with Poland.

The uprising ended in 1658, when Cossacks' Hetman Wyhowski, met with the delegates of the Polish king to sign an agreement that broke the Cossacks-Russia Treaty and established the Republic of Three Nations (Poland, Lithuania, Ukraine), and gave the Cossacks numerous rights. Unfortunately, the settlement was not implemented, and Ukraine fell into a period of devastating wars. In 1667 Ukraine that was entirely part of the Polish-Lithuanian Commonwealth before, was divided between Russia and Poland roughly in half, along the Dnieper river, where its capital Kiev became a Russian city.

The rebellion was a very important event in the history of Ukraine, Poland and Russia. The incorporation of the eastern part of Ukraine into Russia whereby the Cossacks would swear allegiance to the Tsar, while retaining a wide autonomy largely strengthen the empire of the Tsars, and significantly soften the Rzeczpospolita. The success of that anti-Polish rebellion, along with other internal conflicts as well as concurrent wars with Turkey, Russia and Sweden ended the Polish Golden Age causing a decline of Polish power.

Poland-Lithuania vs. Russia

The Mongols ruled today's Russia from 1237 until 1480. Monarchs of the Grand Duchy of Moscow being free immediately started invading neighbouring states. Ivan the Terrible became the first tsar of Russia in 1547 while instituting a reign of terror against nobility using military rule.

In 1558, Ivan launched the Livonian War in an attempt to gain access to the Baltic Sea and its major trade routes. The war took 24 years, engaging the Kingdom of Sweden, the Rzeczpospolita and the Teutonic Knights of Livonia. Ivan the Terrible nearly destroyed his country as the Polish-Lithuanian Commonwealth acquired a talented king, Stefan Batory. King Batory began a series of successful offensives against the Russians in the campaign of 1579–81, and retook major cities of the region. The peace treaty was favourable to the Rzeczpospolita that took most of the Duchy of Livonia (present day Latvia and southern Estonia).

After Ivan the Terrible death in 1584, his son Fyodor was crowned as the tsar. Fyodor took little interest in politics, ruling through Boris Godunov (his closest advisor). Fyodor had only a daughter, and the Rurik dynasty (the Vikings who founded Kiev) which had ruled Russia since the ninth century ended. Godunov was elected as his successor and during his reign Russia experienced so called Time of Troubles (Smuta) at the beginning of XVII century caused by political instability, and a violent succession crisis. It was also ravaged by a great famine and the Polish–Russian War of 1605–1618.

In 1600, a Polish diplomatic mission arrived in Moscow proposing an alliance between Poland and Russia, which would include a future personal union. They proposed that after one monarch's death without heirs, the other would become the ruler of both countries. However, Tsar Godunov declined the union. Meantime many Russian noblemen (boyars), tried to get support from the neighbouring countries to stop ongoing civil war, including the Polish–Lithuanian Commonwealth. Some of them were opportunists thinking about own profits, others looked to their western neighbour, the Rzeczpospolita, and its attractive Golden Freedoms (special privileges that Polish noblemen had), and supported some kind of union between two countries. Other Russian lords tried to tie their fates in alliance with Sweden. The Russians feared that the possible union with the Catholic Poland and Lithuania would endanger Russia's Orthodox traditions and opposed anything that threatened Russian culture, especially education in Polish schools that had already led to successful Polonisation of the Ruthenian lands (Ukrainian) under Polish control.

In 1605 a Russian tsar died and his successor was murdered. Soon a false tsar appeared in Poland claiming his rights to the throne. He got a support from some Polish lords and with their troops and money made his triumphal entry into Moscow, where was crowned Tsar. The following year a conspiracy against new monarch began in Moscow and he was murdered. Then another false tsar appeared (claiming that he avoided the assassination) and also was murdered on Kremlin after a few months.

On July 4, 1610, at the Battle of Klushino near Moscow, the Polish-Lithuanian royal army under Hetman Stanislav Zolkiewski defeated a combined Russian-Swedish force, and Vasily IV was overthrown, and the Russian lords agreed to elevate Polish king's son to the Russian throne. The Poland-Lithuania troops entered Moscow, occupying the city between 1610 and 1612. In a few months riots against invaders began and the Russian Cossacks surrounded the city. The Polish troops in Moscow did not get successful reinforcement from the king and had to surrender. In 1613 a new Russian Tsar Mikhail Romanov was appointed and began reigns of the Romanov dynasty in Russia that lasted till the communist revolution in 1917.

In 1618 Poles tried to conquer Moscow one more time but without success (as the Polish king was still formally a Tsar). In 1619 there was a truce of Deulino that stopped the war till 1632 when the Russians attacked Poland. Then Russia stroke again in 1654. According to the author's count there were 21 wars between both nations in history so far.

In 2004 president Putin re-established the Day of National Unity that the Russians celebrate in remembrance of the Polish intervention. It's a bank holiday in contemporary Russia.

Year 1611 could be considered as probably the apogee of the power of the Polish-Lithuanian Commonwealth. Then there was a Russian tribute - Tsar Wasyl Szujski and his brothers, Dmitri and Ivan, paid tribute to the Polish king and nobility.

At that time, the Commonwealth exercised control over the largest area in its history, and the Polish prince was elected the new tsar of Russia.

On October 29, 1611, a large retinue entered Warsaw, opened by the victorious hussars from the battle of Kluszyno. Behind them, 60 carriages with eminent Lithuanian and Polish families, the field hetman of the crown, rode in the royal carriage, led by six horses. He was followed by prisoners of war in carriages: former Tsar Wasyl IV Szujski with his brothers - Dmitri and Ivan, then the Metropolitan of Rostov Filaret and the defender of Smolensk, voivode Michał Szein. To the cheers of the crowd, the hetman personally led the former ruler of Russia and his siblings to the Senator's Hall at the Royal Castle in Warsaw. There, King Sigismund III, Queen Constanz, Tsar-elect Prince Władysław (the son of the Polish king) and senators awaited them.

At this point, the prisoners bowed to the ground to the king, and then Wasyl IV Szujski kissed the right hand of Sigismund III. Simultaneously, Dimitri hit his head on the floor, and Ivan, in tears, did it three times. Then the hetman asked for a grace for the Szujskis. The ceremony ended with a speech by the Crown Chancellor Feliks Kryski, who praised the achievements of the hetman and called on the nobility to continue financial support for the expeditions in order to maintain the fruits of such a great victory.

With this performance, hetman Żółkiewski showed the enormity of his victory. Convince dignitaries that war should not be skimpy on money, since it brings such effects. The Hetman pointed out: we have conquered Moscow, we have its former ruler who asks for grace in front of our king and his son, the new tsar.

The noble democracy
The Sejm of the Polish nobility did not function effectively. From the mid-seventeenth to the mid-eighteenth century, due to the notorious failure of the parliamentary sessions,

reform attempts focused on strengthening the royal authority but they were unsuccessful, and the monarch's power was gradually more and more limited. As early as 1573, the Sejm introduced the possibility of the nobility renouncing the king's obedience. Such an eventuality was foreseen for the violation of current laws. In practice, denouncing obedience usually took the form of a rebellion. The king became a sort of a lifetime president of decentralised Poland, who could not make any reforms without permission from the Sejm.

In the second half of the XVII century, the domination of the magnates caused that the noble democracy turned into a magnate oligarchy. The powerful magnates who led their coterie became the real rulers of the Rzeczpospolita. With the weakening of royal power, the doctrine of noble equality grew stronger, with its focal point, or "golden freedom". Dozens of magnate families controlling most of the national wealth, divided into factions and competed among themselves keeping the illusion of noble equality as a convenient facade. This system satisfied some of the nobility, but it disorganised the Rzeczpospolita, not serving its interests.

Swedish "Deluge"

At the beginning of XVII century Polish monarch Sigismund III Waza formally became a king of Sweden. Soon his uncle Charles took over the Swedish throne, getting support from many protestant lords who did not want to be ruled by a catholic Sigismund. That triggered the first of the Polish-Swedish wars in 1600-1611 that started in Estonia and brought a series of military victories for the Rzeczpospolita. The Polish hussars defeated much bigger enemy troops in the battle of Kircholm (1605) proving that they were the best military formation in Europe that time. The second war with the Scandinavians in 1626-1629 took place in Pomerania when the victorious Polish fleet destroyed Swedish fleet in the battle of Oliwa. Enemy tried to conquer city of Gdansk – the biggest Polish-Lithuanian port at the Baltic Sea – to control export of goods.

The third war between the countries happened between 1655 and 1660 and is called "Deluge". During five years of war the Commonwealth lost approximately one third of its population as well as its status as a great power. Soon after the Swedish invasion the Rzeczpospolita was also attacked by Russia, Transylvania and Brandenburg and received support from the Kingdom of Denmark. After 1660 (when the peace treaty was signed) the Polish-Lithuanian Commonwealth was a different country – main cities were in ruins, treasury was empty, trade routes disappeared, many provinces entirely lost their population. As a significance of that war, Prussia stopped being a vassal of Poland which had terrible consequences in the upcoming centuries, and the Polish monarch rejected his claims to the Swedish crown. Although the country did not lose its territories it needed urgent and thorough reforms of the parliamentary system, army, treasury, internal and foreign affairs.

The Battle of Vienna

In the summer of 1683, the main army of the Ottoman Empire, a large and well-equipped force, besieged Vienna. The town was nearing the end of its ability to resist: but just as the capture of Vienna was becoming only a matter of time – not more than a week away, at most – an army came to its rescue. On September 12th, in an open battle before Vienna, the Ottoman army was defeated, and the city escaped pillage and destruction. There is probably no book on the general history of Europe that does not record these events. The Chief

Commander of the army that rescued Vienna was the Polish King, Jan Sobieski. He brought with him about 23,000 soldiers, without whom the combined forces of the Emperor and the Imperial princes were not have ventured an open battle. It was only the combination of all three that made victory possible.[28]

The Turks not only threatened Austria but also Poland and Western Europe. Capturing Vienna was a strategic objective of the Ottoman Empire in that time, because the city controlled over Danubian (Black Sea to Western Europe) southern Europe and the overland (Eastern Mediterranean to Germany) trade routes.

According to legend, when the local population emerged from the city to investigate the abandoned Ottoman encampment, they discovered sacks of mysterious dark beans that the invaders had brought with them. And so coffee arrived in Vienna, beginning a long tradition that continues today. Another likely myth is that the siege indirectly gave rise to the croissant. Allegedly, a baker created the crescent-shaped Kipfel to celebrate the victory, a baked item that found its way to Paris in the early 1800s and inspired the creation of that French mainstay.[29]

Economy & Trade

The economy of the Polish-Lithuanian Commonwealth in XVII century was mainly based on agriculture and trade, with a network of workshops and manufactories such as paper mills, leather tanneries, ironworks, glassworks and brickyards.

---

[28] www.historytoday.com/archive/1683-siege-vienna
[29] www.visitingvienna.com/culture/the-1683-siege-of-vienna/

Trade and production of goods were much more developed in the Kingdom of Poland; the Grand Duchy of Lithuania (today's Lithuania, Belarus and Ukraine) was more rural with huge farms and clothmaking. Southern Poland was rich in natural resources such as lead, copper, coal and salt. The currency used in Rzeczpospolita was the same as it is today - the złoty (meaning "the golden"). There were also used and accepted foreign coins: ducats, thalers and others that contained gold or silver. The Baltic city of Gdańsk had the privilege of minting its own coinage. The first Polish banknotes were issued much later, in 1794.

The main export good was grain that was sent to Western Europe in great amount. The country also exported cattle, furs, timber, linen, ash, tar, and amber. Ships from Gdańsk carried cargo to London, Antwerp, Amsterdam and many German ports. Rzeczpospolita imported wine, beer, fruit, exotic spices, luxury goods, furniture, fabrics as well as industrial products like steel and tools.

The wars of the mid-seventeenth century led to enormous damage to the economic potential of cities. The adopted estimation criteria for abandoned houses indicate losses of over 60% in voivodes such as Wielkopolska, Podlasie and Małopolska, and almost 80% in Mazovia and the Ruthenian Voivodeship. Medium and small towns of Royal Prussia, which suffered during the war with Sweden in 1626-29, suffered enormous damage after the Swedish "deluge", and its rich and strong centers such as Gdańsk, Elbląg, Toruń, suffered less, but their income decreased significantly from trade.

The cities that developed dynamically in the Golden Age experienced a rapid economic and demographic collapse during the XVII century. Historians have noticed that already at the end of the symptoms of the impending crisis appeared a century before. One of the main reasons for this was the lack of institutionalised and uniform representation of municipal interests - with the exception of Royal Prussia. The general domestic market of the economy was not quite developed, and Its seeds, such as the towns on the Vistula river, and the relatively well-educated local ones in some regions of the country, did not balance this state of affairs. The crisis of trade in agricultural products in the first quarter of the XVII century and the later elements of the economic crisis of the Polish-Lithuanian Commonwealth, resulting from the period of heavy wars of that century, contributed to the re-feudalisation and rustication of cities. Post-war damage, epidemics and demographic losses cut the vitality of urban organisms. The reluctance of the nobility towards the townspeople, expressed at the sejmiks (regional mini-parliaments) and the Sejm, caused the increase of legal barriers, which made it difficult for cities to carry out their own postulates in parliamentary decision-making bodies, all the conditions and additional factors, such as the negative role of the juridic of the Enlightenment era were in a very difficult general situation.

Chapter 6 – Central Europe in XVIII century

In the first half of the XVIII century the Polish-Lithuanian Commonwealth was in a deep crisis and desperately needed thorough reforms of its parliamentary system, royal court, army, finance, education, home and foreign affairs. The world around diametrically changed, and neighbouring countries – Russia, Prussia and Austria – increased their power significantly, considering weak Poland as a goal of further expansion. The Polish parliament was paralysed, courts were corrupt, unnecessary reforms came very slowly.

The peculiarity of the system of the Polish statehood at the time was that the evolution of the state monarchy did not lead to absolute monarchy, as in the case of the neighbouring powers, but to the creation of a system that was still monarchical, but with essential elements of democracy. And while the erosion of the king's power in the Commonwealth was progressing, democratisation of power and the accompanying decentralisation of sovereignty, efficiently governed European powers built the foundations of modern administration and a standing army. The ratio of forces was most clearly expressed by the size of the army. In the 1760s, the Republic of Poland had 16.000 soldiers, Russia – 350.000, Austria – 280.000, Prussia – 200.000.[30]

In a situation of the threat from the neighbours, a strong, decisive power of the monarch, and alliance with other European countries was absolutely necessary.

In Russia, from the reign of tsar Peter the Great, two concepts regarding Polish-Lithuanian state clashed for a long time: the first aimed at establishing a protectorate over the entire territory of the Rzeczpospolita, the second - its partitions. The second option was chosen in the situation when the ruler of Russia became a Prussian princess (born in the city of Szczecin), known later as Catherine the Great, and when real, state reforms finally took place in Poland in the second half of XVIII century.

The Constitution of 3 May 1791

---

[30] https://publicystyczny.pl/problemy-demokracja-demokracja-szlachecka-pierwszej-rzeczpospolitej/

The Constitution of 1791 was designed to correct the Commonwealth's political faults. It had been preceded by a period of thorough reforms started in 1764 with the election of the last king of Poland - Stanisław August Poniatowski.

It combined a monarchic republic with a clear division of executive, legislative, and judiciary powers, being considered as the first Europe's and the world's second, modern written national constitution, after the United States Constitution of 1789.

It was in force only for nineteen months and happened to be the last will and testament of dying Rzeczpospolita, ending Polish and Lithuanian independence until 1918. Over those 123 years of captivity, the Constitution was a real proof of the Commonwealth's great past and hope for the millions, that one day their motherland would resurrect from dead like Jesus Christ (a concept from XIX century's romanticism).

From now on, only land-owning nobles who were less dependent on the nobility could vote, therefore the possibility of corrupting it was by nature, smaller. This resulted in the elimination of the tool from the hands of the magnates in the form of influencing this part of the nobility and bribing them, so that they could vote in accordance with the indications of individual magnate families, and not necessarily in accordance with the interests of the Polish state.

The Constitution established a hereditary monarchy, so-called "Election by the family". After the future death of King Stanisław August Poniatowski, the throne was to become hereditary and passed over to Frederick Augustus I of the Wettin dynasty, from which the two previous Polish kings came. The highest executive power was entrusted to the Guardians of the Laws, composed of the king, the primate, five ministers, and the adult heir to the throne and the speaker of the Sejm - both without the right to vote. In addition, the size of the army was increased from 16.000 to 65.000.

The Partitions of Poland
The Partitions of Poland were conducted by the Habsburg Monarchy (Austria), the Kingdom of Prussia, and the Russian Empire, which divided up the Rzeczpospolita lands among themselves in 1772, 1793, and 1795, removing the country from the map of Europe.
Long before that, in 1730, these countries signed a secret agreement to maintain the status quo, ensuring that the Rzeczpospolita laws would not change. Their alliance became known in history as the "Alliance of the Three Black Eagles", because all three states used a black eagle as a state symbol (which has a symbolic meaning in contrast to the Polish White Eagle).

Aggressor	% of total area taken from Poland	Population
Russia	62%	7.6m
Prussia	20%	2.6m
Austria	18%	3.8m
Total:	100%	14.0m

The Kościuszko uprising 1794
In 1794 the Kosciuszko uprising took place against the foreign powers that invaded Poland-Lithuania. It was the last chance to protect country's independence, that happened despite the fact that Russia and Prussia were too powerful to be stopped.
General Kościuszko who led the uprising, was an experienced strategist and engineer, one of the American independence

war heroes. He tried to attract to his army all classes of society including peasants, and the middle class, but after two previous partitions, the countries was in deep crisis, already occupied but foreign forces. The general was able to increase his regular army to 55.000, and went to Paris to get support from revolutionary France but without success. After a few great victories, general Kościuszko was unable to defeat the Russian armies before they combined, and badly wounded was imprisoned. Enemy's troops entered Warsaw in Autumn killing, and plundering.

"The Polish-Lithuanian Commonwealth was annihilated not because of internal anarchy, it was annihilated because it tried to reform itself many times," wrote British historian prof. Norman Davies.

Economy & Trade

After a series of damaging wars in XVII century, Poland-Lithuania needed thorough social and economic reforms which did not happen in the first half of the XVIII century when country was ruled by the kings from the Wettin dynasty. King Stanisław August Poniatowski initiated positive changes after his coronation in 1764 together with other patriots in the parliament to heal the Polish economy. They established in line with the Enlightenment idea, the Tax Commission influenced the implementation of the parliamentary act on the abolition of internal customs duties and tolls, which significantly improved the arrangements on the internal market, measures and weights have also been standardised, there was a monetary reform that largely unified and significantly improved the coin. The paper money was implemented the first time in 1794, during the Kościuszko uprising. One of the greatest achievements of the reformers was the introduction of a country budget from 1768, which determined the entire financial management of the state, and was similar to the one in Great Britain. A balanced and increased budget was from now on, a priority for the government and naturally associated with raising taxes, especially on the military, and the newly created areas, such as the civil service, including diplomatic service.

Undoubtedly the greatest role in the field of healing the economy was played by the reforms of the Grand Sejm (1778-1892), including the Constitution of May 3. An extremely difficult political situation of Poland-Lithuania was not favourable for the development of the economy, but there were still patriots who pushed them ahead.

The growing role of cities, towns, and the townspeople was an important factor in the economic reforms. In 1791 the royal cities' townspeople were granted the right to acquire landed estates, hold lower administrative and judicial offices in all courts, and some wealthy townspeople could apply for nobility. Foreign merchants were encouraged to settle in Poland. Peasants were guaranteed the right to freedom of settlement and to hire work.

New government committees were established, such as the Police, the Army, the Treasury, and the National Education.

The economic development of the state specially benefited from the extension of the powers of the Treasury Commission, which dealt with the intensive tax collection, establishing and supporting manufactories, developing trade, building and maintaining roads, floating rivers, and maintaining the post office. Taxes were increased, and in 1789 a permanent tax was levied on noble property.

The significant economic and social reforms strengthen the country on one hand, and caused foreign intervention leading to the collapse of Poland on another. If they happened 50-60 years earlier, Rzeczpospolita probably would have survived.

But in the first half of the century there was nobody to conduct them.

Chapter 7 - Central Europe in XIX century

After the Kosciuszko uprising thousands of Polish patriots had to emigrate abroad, mainly to France, as they were sought by the invaders. Those who did not escaped were persecuted: some were imprisoned or killed, some were sent to Siberia and their properties were confiscated.

Napoleonic Wars

After the third partition of Poland, its leaders on the immigration in Paris started seeking an opportunity to regain independence. In 1797 they persuaded Napoleon Bonaparte to form Polish legions in northern Italy to fight against Austria. In 1807 after successful French campaigns against empires that had partitioned Poland-Lithuania, a tiny state was created in the heart of Europe, the Duchy of Warsaw, that gave the hope to the nation for possible future victory. Unfortunately, The Duchy became a subject of exploitation for the French army, and it was spending 60% of its budget on the French army, supplying thousands of recruits (the Poles formed the largest foreign contingent of 98,000 soldiers in the French army that had around 600,000 troops in total).

In analysing the creation of the Polish Legions, many historians have argued that Napoleon used the Poles as a source of recruits and had little desire to invest in the re-creation of the Polish state. Among the most notable of Napoleon's contemporary Polish detractors was Kosciuszko, who refused to join the Legions, arguing that Napoleon would not restore Poland in any durable form. In this regard, Kosciuszko also stated that the Duchy of Warsaw was created in 1807 only because it was expedient, rather than because Napoleon supported Polish sovereignty. Nevertheless, the memory of Napoleon's Polish Legions is strong in Poland[31]

When in 1812 the French Emperor lost his war against Russia, the Duchy of Warsaw was transformed into The Kingdom of Poland – a small, vassal state of the Russian Empire. It had similar size to Duchy of Warsaw (both were six times smaller than the Polish-Lithuanian Commonwealth) and each Tsar of Russia became automatically the King of Poland during his coronation.

Congress of Vienna

During the Congress of Vienna (1814–1815), which was a conference reconstituting the European political order after the downfall of Napoleon I Bonaparte, main European powers: Great Britain, Russia, Prussia and Austria created a new political system that guaranteed their leadership on the continent, and rules of the empires.

The November Uprising

In 1830 the November uprising took place but the Poles were crashed by powerful empire of Russia. As a punishment, the limited autonomy of the Polish Kingdom was cancelled and its territory became an ordinary province of Russia.

In 1863 the January uprising also did not bring the independence.

Crimean War

---

[31] Norman Davies (2005). God's Playground: A History of Poland in Two Volumes. Oxford University Press. p. 218.

Crimean War between the Russian Empire and the Ottoman Empire and its allies, Great Britain, France and the Kingdom of Sardinia, and was fought in the years 1853–1856. It was triggered by the Russian expansion towards the Balkans, which was threatening not only Turkey but also the British and French trade routes in the Mediterranean. Russia was stopped and the Ottoman Empire did not fall, but it cost lives of 500.000 soldiers. This conflict is considered to be the first war when science and technology had a great influence on the battlefield.

Economy & Trade

The XIX century was a time of dynamic economic changes in the world. At that time, in many countries, especially in Great Britain, there was a wave of modernisation and industrialisation. The economy was driven by John Watt's invention called the steam engine. Significant changes also took place in Poland, although they were disproportionate to the industrialisation of Western Europe. The economic development of the areas of the former Polish-Lithuanian Commonwealth was gradual, often hampered by repressions of the partitioning powers. Nevertheless, it was in a much better position than, the Balkan peninsula, where in many regions medieval farming methods persisted until the end of the XIX century and modern economy was present only in a very few industrial centres.[32]

In the first half of the XIX century the economy of central Europe was based on agriculture, which employed around 80% of the population.

The most develop agriculture was in the Prussian partition of Poland, where the reform of agrarian relations was carried

---

[32] www.historiatomojapasja.blogspot.com

out the earliest, and followed the Prussian laws on the abolition of serfdom and the enfranchisement of peasants. The reforms initiated the formation of the modern structure of agriculture and enabled its conversion to a capitalist economy. Large estates as well as large and medium-sized farms were created, and the growing number of landless people became labourers for the emerging industry. Land consolidation and protection duties intensified agricultural production in the second half of the XIX century, and were comparable to some of those in the most developed European countries.

The situation of agriculture in the Russian partition of Poland was different, and a half of that land was occupied by noble farms, peasants were only users of the land and in return had to do serfdom. In the Austrian partition of Poland was even worse, as the delayed enfranchisement reform did not change the structure of the village, in which apart from noble estates, dominated small farms. They were economically too weak to become modern and efficient.

The process of industrialisation of the Polish lands began in Upper Silesia, where metallurgy and mining of hard coal and iron were developed, and modern technologies covered the entire iron smelting process. Silesia with its sugar, textile, chemical and metal industries had become an important economic center of central Europe. Coal mining increased in the second half of the XIX century to record levels. Industrial cities also developed in Russian and Austrian partitions of Poland with metal industry, and textile industry plants. However, industry was developing later and slower than the one in Prussia.

Trade in central Europe was driven by the development of capitalist relations resulted in the emergence of intermediation, separating the producers from the consumers. Traditional forms of trade on the local markets continued, and the local fairs were places where producers directly delivered their products to consumers and made the necessary purchases themselves.

Large market halls appeared replacing some of the open-air markets and shops.

Modern stock exchanges were not introduced in Polish lands on the same scale as in western countries till 1872, when the Warsaw Stock Exchange was reformed, the goods were removed and only the banker's turnover remained.

In the same year, a grain exchange was established in Warsaw, and in 1879 also a commodity exchange. In spite of that, most of the trading operations still took place outside the stock exchanges. Other Stock Exchanges did not develope as they had big regional competitors such as the Vienna Stock Exchange, where most of the securities were sold.

Chapter 8 - Central Europe in XX century

The Great War 1914-1918

The Great War cost 15 million human lives, finishing unprecedented hegemony of European powers in the world, and starting the world leadership of the United States.

When the heir to the Austrian throne was killed in Sarajevo (the capital of Bosnia) in 1914 nobody expected such a big, global conflict. However, soon Austria-Hungary declared war on Serbia. The Serbian ally, Russia declared war on Austria-Hungary, then the Austrian ally, Germany declared war on Russia and two days later on France. In this situation the French ally, Great Britain declared war on Germany. Russia attacked Turkey, and Italy declared war on Austria-Hungary.

In 1914, Europe was no longer ruled by dynasties, but by rival political and military blocs. Each of them wanted to increase their territory, increase their importance and increase their power. The outbreak of World War I showed that the numerous dynastic and family ties between the ruling European houses were no longer of any importance. The European countries joining the war were aware of the inevitable and large loss of life.[33]

The first time the empires that participated in the partitions of Poland-Lithuania in the XVIII century, began fighting against each other: Germany and Austria against Russia. That was a great chance for the Polish, Lithuanians and other nations of Central and Eastern Europe to regain their independence. The price of freedom was very high but definitely it was worth of that. When the USA with its almost unlimited resources, joined Britain and France in 1917, it became clear that Germany and its allies could not win the war. The Germans failed with their strategic plan to defeat France by a surprise attack, using a rapid, overwhelming force concentration, and they had to fight simultaneously with Russia on the east front too. The situation changed in Central and Eastern Europe when the hardship of the war helped communists to take control over Russia. The communists killed the tsar and signed a peace treaty with Germany, recognising Russian defeat. A bloody civil war between new communist regime and tsar's loyalists was continued in Russia. On 11 November 1918 the war was over. New countries gained (re-gained) their independence: from the ruins of the Russian empire emerged Poland, Lithuania, Latvia and Estonia; from the Austro-

---

[33] Theo Aronson, Warring Monarchs The Triumph and Tragedy of European Monarchies in 1910–1918, ed. Polish 1998, pp. 114, 118.

Hungarian empire emerged Czechoslovakia, Austria, Hungary, and Yugoslavia.

After the great war, Poland and Lithuania became separate states and the glorious idea of the Commonwealth could not be continued anymore. However, the father of Polish independence -Marshal Pilsudski - tried to create the Intermarium – the Rzeczpospolita's successor. He predicted that another conflict with Russia is only a matter of time, and he tried to use the civil war in Russia to sign a peace treaty that guarantee fragile Polish independence.

The Polish–Soviet war 1919-21

The Polish–Soviet war last between February 1919 and March 1921, and was fought on territories formerly held by Russia and Austria-Hungary and that used to belong to the Polish-Lithuanian Commonwealth before the partitions. The Soviets under rule of Lenin saw Poland as the bridge that the Red Army had to cross to spread the communist revolution to all Europe, especially to Germany. Pilsudski believed that the best way for Poland to secure its borders was by military action and decided to conquer the capital of Ukraine Kiev. He was ready to march with his troops to Moscow but soon the Polish offensive was met by a successful Red Army counterattacks and the Poles had to retreat. Great Britain and France started fear that soon the Soviet troops would arrive at Germany as in August 1920 the fall of Warsaw seemed to be unavoidable. Then the Polish forces achieved an unexpected and decisive victory at the Battle of Warsaw, crushing the Soviet armies led by Stalin and Tukhachevsky which resulted in the Soviets' proposal for peace, and the war ended with a ceasefire.

The Treaty of Versailles 1919

The Treaty of Versailles signed in June 1919 finished the great war, and Germany accepted its responsibility for causing all the loss and damages.

In central Europe Germany were forced to cede parts of the province of Upper Silesia to Czechoslovakia and Poland. The province of Poznań and Eastern Pomerania (taken previously by Prussia in XVIII century) came back to Poland. City of Gdansk on the Baltic coast became the Free City of Gdansk and another Baltic port, Memel, came back to Lithuania.

Belarus (in the past Duchy of Polotsk – a medieval principality) and Ukraine (Kievan Rus in the Middle Ages) did not have a strong leadership to gain independence but at least gained some autonomy as the Soviet republics.

League of Nations

In 1920 the USA proposed to create the League of Nations (predecessor of the United Nations), that was the first international organisation whose principal mission was to maintain world peace. The League has a mixed record of solving disputes between countries, sometimes contending with governments that did not recognised its authority. Many times it helped to resolve issues in central and eastern Europe in spite of the fact that Soviet Union was a member of the League only between 1934 and 1939 (when was expelled), and Germany was a member only between 1926 and 1933. Even more importantly, the USA never joined the League which was the main weakness of the organisation.

Rapallo 1922

In 1922 Germany and Soviet Union signed the Treaty of Rapallo which strengthen their cooperation and mutually renounced claims to compensation for military costs and non-military losses. Germany was the first nation that established a diplomatic relations with the first communist state in world. Such agreement was a serious threat for the Polish independence and marshal Pilsudski as a leader of Poland strengthened the military alliance with France, and tried to do the same with Great Britain and neighbouring countries such as Romania.

Poland signed non-aggression pacts with the Soviet Union in 1932 and with Germany in 1934, but both were broken by those powers in September 1939.

Hitler became a new German chancellor in 1933

Many historians believe that the period between 1918 and 1939 was just a short break (a geopolitical pause) between two parts of the same global conflict. Local disputes between nations in central and eastern Europe last all that period, and were caused by the fact that nobody was satisfied with the shape of new borders, countries were devastated by the war, societies were very poor, unemployment was high. All this with the rise of communism in Russia and fascism in Germany made international affairs very difficult in 1930s.

Hitler became a new German chancellor in 1933, and from the very first day began his aggressive policy to give Germany economic and political domination. He saw Jews, communists and the Soviet Union as German greatest enemies, and central and eastern Europe as lands for German expansion and exploitation. Hitler's strategy in the 1930s was to make (in his opinion) sensible demands, and then if they were not met, he threated the country of war. When opponents tried to satisfy him, he accepted the offered gains and moved to the next goal. That aggressive strategy functioned as Germany pulled out of the League of Nations, rejected the Versailles Treaty, and began to rearm. After retaking the Saar Basin, Germany remilitarised the Rhineland, formed an alliance with Italy, and imperial Japan.

In 1934 Germany tried to seize Austria first time. The country was considered to be a German state, and was a place where Hitler was born (Vienna).

The Austrian Chancellor, Dollfuss, tried to crack down on the Socialists and Nazis - political factions that he thought were tearing the country apart, and soon he banned the Nazi party. Hitler ordered the Austrian Nazis to create chaos in Austria, which turned into an attempt to overthrow the Austrian government. Chancellor Dollfuss was murdered but the attempted coup failed because the Austrian military intervened to back up the government.

Italy signed an agreement with Austria in 1934 that would protect Austria from outside aggression. The Italian dictator, Mussolini, moved Italian troops to the Austrian border to deter Hitler from possible invading. The new Austrian Chancellor, Schuschnigg tried to preserve the country from German invasion by trying not to give Hitler an excuse for aggression, and co-operating with him as much as possible. Schuschnigg signed the German-Austrian Agreement of 1936 that recognised the independence of Austria but the price was that Austria's foreign policy had to be consistent with Germany's. The agreement also allowed Nazis to hold official posts in Austria. Schuschnigg hoped this would appease Hitler. He was wrong.[34]

---

[34] www.bbc.co.uk/bitesize/guides/z92hw6f/revision/3

In March 1938 the German troops and Hitler himself entered Austria and were greeted by loud cheers. One month later, 99% of Austrians voted in favour of the annexation of their country to the Nazi-Germany. France and Great Britain were not in a position to oppose Hitler which only encouraged him to get more. As a result of the annexation of Austria, Germany gained 7 million people and 100,000 Austrian troops that they added to its own, increasing their influence in the Balkans, and central Europe.

Soon Czechoslovakia (surrounded on three fronts by Germany) became Hitler's main target. He demanded autonomy for the Germans who lived in areas near the Czecho-German borders (so called Sudetenland) and then wanted annexation of these territories. In May 1938 the government in Prague announced a partial mobilisation facing possible German invasion. The Czechoslovak army was very modern and had an excellent system of frontier fortifications on the border with Germany. Then Hitler signed a secret directive to begin war against Czechoslovakia, and gave a speech in the German parliament persuading that his territorial claims are the last ones. In September 1938 in Munich, leaders of Great Britain, France, Italy and Germany signed an agreement that sanctioned partitions of Czechoslovakia.

Winston Churchill said to the ruling British Prime Minister Chamberlain soon after the Munich Conference:

"You were given the choice between war and dishonour. You chose dishonour, and you will have war."

The Nazi-Germany conquered Sudetenland, and Hitler's appetite for new lands grew even faster. In March 1939 he ordered his troops to take rest of Czechoslovakia, and his generals started planning war against Poland.

Hitler stressed the military importance of occupation, noting that by occupying Czechoslovakia, Germany gained 2.175 field cannons, 469 tanks, 500 anti-aircraft artillery pieces, 43.000 machine guns, 1.090.000 military rifles, 114.000 pistols, about a billion rounds of ammunition and three million anti-aircraft shells. This amount of weaponry would be sufficient to arm about half of the then Wehrmacht.[35]

Czechoslovak weaponry later played a major part in the Nazi-Germany attacks on other European countries.

In March 1939 Germany took over Lithuanian Baltic port of Klaipeda (Memel), and two months later demanded from Poland an exterritorial highway from Pomerania to Prussia through Polish territory, together with Polish acceptance for German annexation of the Free City of Gdansk.

The Polish Foreign Minister Beck firmly refused these demands replying:

"Peace is a precious and desirable thing. Our generation, trained in wars, certainly deserves a period of peace, but peace, like almost all matters of this world, has its price, high, but measurable. We in Poland do not know the concept of peace at any cost!".

This cost Poland over 6 million casualties during the Second World War, and some people still believe that the price of peace was too high.

Hitler after becoming the chancellor of Germany wanted Poland to be his main ally in the German crusade against the Soviet Union, but anti-communist governments in Warsaw were aware of the fact that Nazi-Germany are same kind of evil as The Soviet Union and for many years tried to balance between those powerful enemies. When Great Britain

---

[35] Motl, Stanislav (2007), *Kam zmizel zlatý poklad republiky* (2nd ed.), Prague: Rybka publishers

decided to guarantee Polish independence Hitler was surprised of that and delayed his plans to attack Poland from 26th August to 1st September 1939.

Beginning of the Second World War

In June 1939 outstanding Polish intellectualist Władysław Studnicki wrote a brochure: "In view of the coming World War II" where he criticised military alliance with Great Britain as he predicted that London would bring the Soviet Union to war to defeat Nazi-Germany and then the price for it will be eastern Poland. But who else could be better allies than Britain and France – powerful world leaders? The only counter option was an alliance with the Soviets, that was not considered whatsoever.

23 August 1939 German Foreign Minister Ribbentrop met with Soviet Foreign Minister Molotov in Moscow to sign the agreement between their country that neither the Soviet Union nor Nazi Germany would attack each other.

A secret part established spheres of interest in eastern Europe, and a border between both countries existed after they had invaded and divided Poland.[36]

The secret annex specified that the Baltic states (Latvia and Estonia) and Finland will become the sphere of influence and the future territory of the Soviet Union, and the northern border of Lithuania is to be the border between the zones of interest between Germany and the Soviet Union. In the areas belonging to the Polish state, the districts of interest of Germany and the Soviet Union will be bordered along the

---

[36] Fisher, David & Read, Anthony 1999. The Deadly Embrace: Hitler, Stalin, and the Nazi–Soviet Pact 1939–1941. New York: W.W. Norton & Co.

lines of the Vistula, Narew and San rivers (almost exactly in the middle of Poland).

The Soviet Union expressed its interest to seize Bessarabia (Moldova), while the Germans gave the green light to the Soviets in that territory.

American diplomat Bohlen wrote in his diaries that the content of the secret protocol was known to the US government the following day. The Americans informed about it the British Foreign Office, and Great Britain shared it with France soon after. Poland and other countries who were victims of the agreement were not informed.

First of September 1939 Germany attacked Poland in agreement with the Soviet Union. That day, which is considered to be the first day of the Second World War, Poland had a military alliance with France, Great Britain, and Romania. Germany was bound by the anti-Comintern pact with Japan and Italy. Formally, the war became a global conflict when Great Britain and France declared war on Germany on 3rd September. However, neither Italy nor Japan joined the war on the side of Germany at this stage, Hungary and Romania announced neutrality.

The Nazi-Germany used the "blitzkrieg" strategy that help them break the Polish borders in the first days of the war. The invading armies showed their absolute dominance in the air and their superiority of technology over Polish, and it was not possible to put up an effective resistance. The difficult situation of the Polish army was not changed by several single victories of the Polish troops (e.g. the Battle of Mokra). The Germans reached Warsaw on 8th September, which they began to besiege. The biggest battle of the campaign took place on the Bzura River where fought 650.000 soldiers on both sides, and the Poles suffered very heavy losses.

On 17th September without a declaration of war specified in international law, Poland was also attacked by the Soviet Union.

On 28th September Warsaw was capitulated and on 6th October, the last battle of the campaign ended - the Battle of Kock.

The inhabitants of both occupied parts of the Polish state were repressed by the occupiers.

As early as September 1939, the underground state structures subordinated to the Polish Government in Exile began to operate, the state of the Republic of Poland was preserved in the international arena, and the Polish underground administration and the underground army were recreated in the occupied country.

Germany and the Soviet Union demarcated their border in the occupied Polish territory.

The Soviets annexed the Baltic states in 1940, and sent an ultimatum to Finland demanding to accept Russian military bases on its territory and annexation of some Finish territories. Finland refused and the Soviet Union attacked that northern state (November 1939), and although the Finnish forces were much weaker than the aggressor, they managed to stop the Red Army. The Finns inflicted huge losses on the Red Army (127.000 killed and missing) against their own (30.000 killed), and defended its independence.

When the Battle of Britain began in July 1940 the British had fewer fighters than the Germans - the British 800 fighters, and the Germans 1000. Germany had an even greater advantage in the number of bombers – 1.500 planes against 400 British bombers. However, in the next months the British industry produced 1.900 machines, and it got to the point where there was no one to fly them, so they had to use pilots from other countries. 2.900 airmen from 14 countries fought in the Battle of Britain in total, including 144 from Poland, and 84 from Czechoslovakia, who proved very effective in the air. The Poles shot down 203 Germans planes, and Czech Josef Frantisek scored 17 downed planes (the Germans lost 1.733 planes in the Battle of Britain in total).

Also Polish navy took part in protecting the British coasts during the war. Three destroyers and two submarines left Poland in September 1939 and joined the British Navy. The entire operating costs of the Polish fleet were covered by the Polish government on exile. They have 8 confirmed and 5 probable sinkings, as well as 11 confirmed and 18 probable damage to German ships. The Polish Navy also took part in the largest landing operation in World War II - the Normandy landings (D-Day).

In 1939–1941, the Soviet Union conducted intensive economic cooperation with Germany on the basis of the Molotov-Ribbentrop Pact, and relations between the two countries remained friendly. However, Hitler was preparing a plan to invade the Soviet Union, long before it happened in June 1941. In September 1941 the Germans reached Moscow, as the Russian capital was the most important target for the invaders, and its collapse would be a great military, and political success. However, Moscow was very well fortified and its garrison was supplied with reserve armies from Siberia and the Far East. The Germans failed to capture the city as the fights dragged on and lost the character of the Blitzkrieg ("lightning war") that the invaders were trying to wage. The winter of 1941/1942 was the most severe in the XX century, and the temperature often dropped to -45 °C. Such weather was deadly for armoured equipment that was not adapted to winter fights, and what more important, the German infantry did not have warm uniforms.

In January 1944, the Soviet troops crossed the former Polish border, in June launched a strategic offensive in Belarus defeating the main German Army, and reached the Vistula river.

In August 1944, the Warsaw Uprising broke out, initiated by the Home Army (Armia Krajowa) in order to seize the capital of Poland before the initiation of the Red Army. After 63 days of heroic fighting, the uprising collapsed, not receiving any help from the Soviets who stopped their offensive on the right side of Vistula.

In January 1945, another Soviet offensive was launched, which drove the Germans from the Vistula River to the fortifications of the Pomeranian Wall and the rivers Odra and Nysa (present-day Polish-German border).

The Soviets after the occupation of Romania entered the territory of Hungary and Yugoslavia. Belgrade was liberated in October 1944, and Budapest in February 1945. A month later, Soviet-Bulgarian forces captured Vienna. On 7th of May Nazi-Germany capitulated in Berlin, and thus, World War II in Europe officially ended.

For many years after the war, on the occupied by the Soviet Union territories, organised groups of patriots fought against the communists: in Poland so-called the "Cursed Soldiers" (Żołnierze Wyklęci), and in the Baltic states the "Forest Brothers".

Nazi-Germany have committed numerous war crimes, particularly in central and eastern Europe where they established many concentration camps, which were an instrument of genocide of conquered nations.

Nazi-Germany, as part of a deliberate program of extermination, systematically killed over 11 million people including 6 million Jews (Holocaust) and 500.000 Gypsies (Porajmos).

About 75 million people died in World War II, including about 20 million soldiers and 40 million civilians, many of whom died because of deliberate genocide, massacres, mass-bombings, disease, and starvation. The Soviet Union lost 27 million people, Poland 6 million, Germany 5.3 million, Yugoslavia 1.7 million, Greece 0.8 million, Czechoslovakia 0.4 million, Lithuania 0.4 million.

The Soviet Union was responsible for the Katyn massacre of 22.000 Polish officers in 1940 and the imprisonment or execution of thousands of political prisoners in the Baltic states and eastern Poland annexed by the Red Army.

In addition to Nazi concentration camps, the Soviet gulags (labour camps) led to the deaths of 3.6 million people.[37]

New post-war world was shaped at conferences in Teheran, Yalta and Potsdam where the leaders of the world powers met.

The alliance between the United Kingdom, the United States and the Soviet Union had initially operated via correspondence and a series of bilateral conferences. As the war progressed, however, plans were made to bring the heads of government of these three allied powers together to discuss key issues arising from the conflict.[38]

At the Tehran conference, held in the Iranian capital in November and December 1943, the UK Prime Minister Winston Churchill, US President Franklin Roosevelt and Soviet

---

[37] courses.lumenlearning.com/suny-hccc-worldhistory2/chapter/casualties-of-worldwarii/#:~:text=Some%2075%20million%20people%20died,bombings%2C%20disease%2C%20and%20starvation.

[38] https://lordslibrary.parliament.uk/tehran-yalta-and-potsdam-three-wartime-conferences-that-shaped-europe-and-the-world/

Premier Joseph Stalin met together for the first time in person to discuss military strategy and the post-war world order. The Yalta conference, held on the Crimean coast in February 1945. The last of the three major war summits was the conference in Potsdam (the southwest of Berlin) in July and August 1945, after Germany's unconditional surrender.

The Americans, British and Russians have decided there that central and eastern Europe would be dominated by the Soviet Union: the Baltic states Lithuania, Latvia, and Estonia (previously independent countries) became Soviet republics, the eastern half of Poland was incorporated to the Soviet Union, and the Poles received western part of Germany as the compensation of the lost territories (the Polish government was forced to accept it), Bessarabia (Moldova) became a Soviet republic, a part of Czechoslovakia was annexed to the Soviet Union. That was the price that had to be paid to the Soviet Union for its engagement in defeating Nazi-Germany.

Cold War 1945-1990

The Beginning of the Cold War started shortly after ending the World War II. That new era was a shift in global leadership, when the old great powers such as France and Great Britain declined, and the world became dominated by two superpowers: the Soviet Union and the USA.

The Allies established occupation administrations in Germany, dividing it into occupation zones, processing a denazification, and prosecuting Nazi war criminals.

Growing hostility between the western and communist blocs resulted in establishing NATO in 1949 with its headquarters in Brussels, and the Warsaw Pact in 1955. Both military pacts officially had a defensive character but their plans for a possible war where quite offensive, and assumed nuclear confrontation if one of the members would be attacked.

Two economic blocs were also created: The Council for Mutual Economic Assistance (COMECON) in 1949 with headquarters in Moscow, and the European Coal and Steel Community in 1952, that later became the European Union.

In 1956 the Hungarian Revolution broke in Budapest, and was directed against the communist regime and its Soviet masters, The revolt began as a student protest, which attracted thousands of people. Disorder and violence erupted for several months throughout the capital, the government collapsed, and the Russian tanks entered Budapest.

Prague Spring.

In 1968 mass protests took place in the Czechoslovak Socialist Republic which are known as the Prague Spring. They were caused primarily by the social and economic crisis that was increasingly overwhelming Czechoslovakia as a result of the destruction of the central planning economy promoted in the country after the war. The groups of protesters (mainly intellectuals) called for deep reforms and changes in the government. The Soviet Union recognised the Prague Spring as an anti-Communist movement threatening its position in central Europe, and decide to send the Warsaw Pact troops to Prague. As a result of the Spring, thousands of people were fired from their jobs, many emigrated, and some activists were imprisoned. Society withdrew into the sphere of private life until the Velvet Revolution in 1989.

The pope John Paul II

Polish cardinal Karol Wojtyła became the pope John Paul II in 1978 and stayed the head of the Catholic Church until 2005.

With the beginning of his pontificate the first signs of the Soviet Union future collapse had appeared, and the pope's role in bringing down Communism in central and eastern Europe seems to be significant, especially as the spiritual leader for millions of believers. Lech Wałęsa, the President of Poland in 1990-1995, said that before his pontificate, the world was divided into blocs, and nobody knew how to get rid of Communism.

In June 1979, John Paul II went on his first pilgrimage to Poland, where he said during his visit:

"I am calling, I, the son of Polish land, and at the same time I, John Paul II, the Pope. I cry from all the depths of this Millennium, I cry on the eve of Pentecost, I cry with all of you: Let Your Spirit descend! Let Your Spirit descend and renew the face of the earth. This land!".

Solidarity movement

Solidarity movement was founded in 1980 in Poland and was the first independent trade union in the Warsaw Pact country. The union reached 10 million members in the following year, becoming a great anti-Communist movement demanding workers' rights, using civil resistance methods. The communists attempted to destroy the union through the imposition of martial law, and political repressions in Poland. The movement survived and Solidarity's leader Lech Wałęsa was awarded the Nobel Peace Prize in 1983 and the union is widely respected for its central role in the end of communism in Europe.

In 1989 the agreement between the communist government and the Solidarity led to first free parliamentary election after the Word War II in the Eastern bloc. The next year Lech Wałęsa was elected President of Poland.

Economy & Trade

At the turn of the XIX and XX centuries new economic processes in central Europe, such as the transition from free competition to monopolisation with cartels and corporations, big financial capital emerged, return to protectionism, and the gold currency system.

They could not remain without influence on the formation of capitalism in reborn Poland, and other countries of central Europe.

Huge war damages as a result of the front line shifting several times in many areas of Poland, caused that the level of economic development was much lower than in western Europe.

The shaping of the economic system of Poland in this period was a slow process as Poland gradually developed. The borders with Russia were established in 1921, in 1922 Silesia was annexed to Poland, and years 1918-1923 were the period of the war economy.

The percentage of foreign ownership was high after World War I and the policy of the state was focused on attracting foreign capital. However, this capital did not create the so-called green field investments. It was buying shares of already existing enterprises. In 1927, foreign capital constituted 21%, and in 1934 47% of the equity of Polish joint-stock companies. Regarding the role of the market and the state, the state sector was strong, and continued to grow after the crisis in 1930s, with

the years in which the indirect influence of the state on the economy dominated.

In 1921 Poland started building its main Baltic port from scratch. The investment was primarily to facilitate the economic development of the country under construction (maritime trade), but also to contribute to increasing the state's defence capabilities. From the very beginning, the momentum of the project itself, its enormous scale and innovation, as well as the lightning-fast pace of the work were impressive. Gdynia became a symbol of the modernisation ambitions and investment effort of the Second Polish Republic.

Deputy Prime Minister Eugeniusz Kwiatkowski initiated in 1936 Central Industrial District (COP) - an industrial district in central Poland, between the Vistula, Dunajec and San rivers. The COP was also built from scratch or expanded the existing heavy, armaments, machinery and agricultural industries. The constructions of a hydroelectric dam, a power plant, a steelworks and many other great industrial projects were part of the plans to make Poland one of the leading European economic powers. Unfortunately, the Second War stopped those brave plans, and the Soviet Union had own plans to introduce communism in central European countries after the war.

Under Russian occupation Polish economy in 1940s switched to a socialist system with radical changes in the sphere of ownership and regulations. In 1950s there was an attempt to introduce the Soviet model with a strong industrialisation as well as further nationalisation, and collectivisation. In 1960s and 1970s there was a time of stabilisation of the economic system, that finished with a big social and economic crises, Solidarity movement, and finally with the martial law in 1981. The collapse of the system of real socialism in 1989 began the period of the complete and comprehensive transformation of the system from a centrally planned economy to a market economy in all countries of Central and Eastern Europe.

Chapter 9 – New Intermarium (XXI century)

NATO and EU

In 1999 Poland, Hungary, and the Czech Republic as first Central and Eastern European countries joined NATO, followed by Lithuania, Latvia, Estonia, Romania, Slovakia, Bulgaria, and Slovenia in 2004; Albania and Croatia in 2009, Montenegro in 2017, and North Macedonia in 2020.
Bosnia and Herzegovina, Georgia and Ukraine are official candidates to join NATO, and in several countries such as Sweden, Finland, and Serbia, joining this military organisation is currently a topic of political debate, and it has been a cause of increased tension between NATO members and Russia.
After collapsing the Soviet Union, joining the European Union also became a primary goal for central European states, equally important as joining NATO.
They wanted to join the European integration seeking the economic success and a guarantee that they did not fall back into the Russian sphere of influence again. It was a long and difficult process but after reunification of Germany, the Czech Republic, Poland, Estonia, Hungary, Latvia, Lithuania, Slovakia, and Slovenia, together with Malta and Cyprus joined the EU in May 2004. Romania and Bulgaria joined the EU a bit later, in 2007.

Russian aggression on Ukraine and Georgia

So called the Orange Revolution took place in Ukraine in 2004. It was a series of protests, civil disobedience, and strikes that started after the presidential election, which was claimed to be massively corrupted. The protests resulted in more than 100 casualties, and took out Ukraine from the Russian sphere of influence. Soon, officials supporting ties with Russia started military actions in Eastern and Southern Ukraine alluding to the possibility of the disintegration of the country.

In 2014 Ukrainian region of Donbas became a place of an armed conflict, where Russian separatists self-declared a People's Republic, which was followed by Russian annexation of the Crimea. Russia took advantage of unrest in Ukraine launching a political and military campaign against Ukraine, supporting pro-Russian unrest by employing so called the hybrid war (a combination of disinformation tactics, irregular fighters, regular Russian troops, and other military support to destabilise that country). Ukraine launched a military counter-offensive against pro-Russian forces, and then the Russians abandoned their tactics, and began a conventional invasion of the region with artillery, and personnel crossing the Ukrainian border. There is no chance for finishing that conflict, and returning the Crimea to Ukraine in the near future.

In August 2008 Russian troops invaded Georgia (that regained its independence in 1991). Following the election of Vladimir Putin in Russia in 2000 and Georgian plans to join NATO, relations between Russia and Georgia reached a full diplomatic crisis. Pro-Russian separatists in South Ossetian region started shooting Georgian villages, and the Georgian army intervention was necessary, which became an excuse for the Russian attack. The Russian aggression was a large-scale land, air and sea invasion and was called in Moscow a "peace enforcement" operation.

During the Russo-Georgian War a series of cyberattacks swamped and disabled websites of numerous South Ossetian, Georgian, Russian and Azerbaijani organisations. The attacks were initiated three weeks before the shooting war began in what is regarded as "the first case in history of a coordinated cyberspace domain attack synchronized with major combat actions in the other warfighting domains (consisting of Land, Air, Sea, and Space)."[39]

Presidents of Poland, Lithuania, Estonia, Ukraine and the prime minister of Latvia, met with Georgian president at 12 August 2008 in Tbilisi showing their full support to Georgian independence and integrity in front of the parliament where also gathered 200.000 Georgians patriots, enthusiastically responding to the Polish president Lech Kaczyński's speech. He said among other things: "Central Europe has courageous leaders. And I would like to say this not only to you. I would also like to say to those from our common European Union that Central Europe, Georgia, that our entire region will be important, that we are the entity. (...) And we also know very well that today Georgia, tomorrow Ukraine, then the Baltic states, and soon maybe it's time for my country, for Poland - warned President Kaczyński. - We believe that Europe will understand Georgian right to freedom, its own interests, and that Russia wants to restore its empire, which is in no one's interest. That's why we're here."

The war was stopped and a cease fire agreement was signed, owing to active support from central European states, European Union and the USA, but currently about 20% of Georgia's internationally recognised territory is under Russian military occupation.

---

[39] Hollis, David (6 January 2011). "Cyberwar Case Study: Georgia 2008" (PDF). Small Wars Journal.

President Kaczyński died on 10 April 2010 in a plane crash on the Russian Federation territory, together with other members of a Polish delegation flying from Warsaw to commemorate the Katyn massacre. The plane crashed while approaching Smolensk Air Base in Russia. 96 people were killed in the crash, including many of Poland's highest military and civilian leaders.

Economy & Trade

In 2001 the Euro (currency of European Union) was introduced in by Austria, Belgium, Finland, France, Germany, Greece, Ireland, Italy, Luxembourg, the Netherlands, Portugal, and Spain. The new currency is considered by many economists as a good tool to support economic growth, low unemployment, and stability of prices. Some of the 3SI nations also decided to implement the new currency and joined the monetary union: Slovenia (2007), Slovakia (2009), Estonia (2011), Latvia (2014), and Lithuania (2015). Other countries such as Hungary also see lots of benefits from using the Euro, however recent economic crises in Southern Europe (e.g. in Greece) clearly shown that in the time of economic instability, having its own currency can be a great advantage.

The beginning of the XXI century have brought a significant improvement in the life of 3SI societies. This is the effect of the systemic reforms, joining the EU, NATO and other international organisations. However, the world changes, and further reforms are needed to continue the 3SI nations economic success.

PART 4 Extras

MAPS

M0 – Central Europe in 1815

ICELAND
NORWAY
SWEDEN
DENMARK
RUSSIAN EMPIRE
UNITED KINGDOM OF GREAT BRITAIN AND IRELAND
NETHERLANDS
GERMAN EMPIRE
BELGIUM
LUXEMBOURG
FRENCH REPUBLIC
SWITZERLAND
LIECHTENSTEIN
AUSTRO-HUNGARIAN EMPIRE
ROMANIA
SAN MARINO
MONACO
KINGDOM OF ITALY
SERBIA
BULGARIA
MONTENEGRO
ALBANIA
OTTOMAN EMPIRE
GREECE
PORTUGAL
SPAIN
CYPRUS

ICELAND
FINLAND
SWEDEN
NORWAY
ESTONIA
LATVIA
LITHUANIA
USSR
DENMARK
IRELAND
UNITED KINGDOM
NETHERLANDS
BELGIUM
LUXEMBOURG
GERMAN REICH
POLAND
CZECHOSLOVAK REPUBLIC
LIECHTENSTEIN
HUNGARY
ROMANIA
SWITZERLAND
FRENCH REPUBLIC
ITALY
SAN MARINO
YUGOSLAVIA
BULGARIA
MONACO
ANDORRA
PORTUGAL
SPAIN
ALBANIA
GREECE
TURKEY
CYPRUS

Economic success of Central Europe - 1989-2021

War reparations from Germany were never fully paid to central European countries that suffered huge losses after World War II, despite of the fact that the Federal Republic of Germany and the German Democratic Republic were obliged to pay them. For example, as a result of the aggression of Nazi Germany, a large part of Poland was subjected to enormous destruction. 62% of the industry was destroyed, infrastructure 85%, and about 17% of the population lost their lives during the war.

It is worth remembering that some reparations Germany paid to the Soviet Union – at the Yalta Conference, it was agreed that the total amount of reparations that Germany would have to pay would be $20 billion (the value of the 1938 dollar). Of this amount, the Soviet Union have received half. 15 percent of this amount was to go to Poland, but it has not been transferred.

Central Europe that after the Second War was part of the Soviet bloc, under pressure from Moscow did not participate in the Marshall plan, which was a U.S.-sponsored program designed to rehabilitate the economies of European countries. It was also called the European Recovery Program, and from 1947 provided economic assistance to restore the economic infrastructure of postwar Europe. The United States transferred over $13 billion that had a very positive impact on the seventeen countries, triggering fast economic growth. This $13.2 billion that the US dedicated to the Plan from 1948 to 1952 would be worth a substantial $135 billion in today's money. Only Austria among all today's 3SI countries took part in the Marshall plan.

Economic recovery in eastern Europe was much slower than in the west, and economies did not fully recover during the communism, resulting in a a gap between West and East prosperity. Without the Marshall Plan funds, industrial production in Poland, Hungary, Bulgaria and Czechoslovakia exceeded the pre-war level by 1948.

Conclusion and recommendations for the 3SI

New transport routes, especially from North to South are needed, with big, modern ports on the Baltic Sea, the Black Sea and the Adriatic Sea coasts, network of motorways (railways), and at least one large airport to facilitate multi-directional trade.

Hopefully, the USA and the UK will help develop the 3SI in a long perspective by providing financial and political support, competing in the region with the Chinese 16+1 format. Otherwise CEE might be reduced to the role of a lever that creates Germany's geopolitical power in the world, and a recipient of Chinese goods.

A potential Three Seas crisis in connection with the possible withdrawal of the United States from political support. In this approach, the transaction price paid by Washington for taking over the key role in ensuring the security of Europe by Germany is the withdrawal of its opposition to Nord Stream and consent to the takeover of the Three Seas Initiative by Germany. Another risk for the 3SI is the consent to the takeover of the Three Seas project by Germany in exchange for maintaining the Euro-Atlantic course of the European Union and ensuring the security of Ukraine. That in both key issues would have direct impact on Polish national security.

www.ingramcontent.com/pod-product-compliance
Lightning Source LLC
Chambersburg PA
CBHW051600250726

48653CB00004BA/1242